Donna Kooler's
555 Cross-Stitch Patterns
for the Young
at Heart

Sterling Publishing Co., Inc. New York
A Sterling/Chapelle Book

Chapelle Ltd.

Owner: Jo Packham

Editor: Karmen Quinney

Staff: Areta Bingham, Kass Burchett, Marilyn Goff, Holly Hollingsworth, Susan Jorgensen, Kimberly Maw, Barbara Milburn, Linda Orton, Leslie Ridenour, Cindy Stoeckl, Gina Swapp, Kim Taylor, Sara Toliver, Kristi Torsak

Photography: Kevin Dilley/Hazen Photo Studio

Kooler Design Studio, Inc.

President: Donna Kooler

Vice President & Editor: Priscilla Timm

Executive Vice President: Linda Gillum

Staff Designers: Barbara Baatz, Linda Gillum, Nancy Rossi, Jorja Hernandez, Sandy Orton, Thomas Taneyhill, Pam Johnson

Design Assistants: Sara Angle, Anita Forfang, Laurie Grant, Virginia Hanley-Rivett, Marsha Hinkson, Arlis Johnson, Char Randolph, Karen Million, Connie Regner, Kim Goodrum, Giana Shaw

Library of Congress Cataloging-in-Publication Data

Kooler, Donna.
    Donna Kooler's 555 cross-stitch patterns for the young at heart / Donna Kooler.
        p. cm.
    Includes index.
    ISBN 0-8069-7188-6
    1. Cross-stitch–Patterns. 2. Samplers. 3. Nursery rhymes in art. I. Title:
555 cross-stitch patterns for the young at heart. II. Title.

TT778.C76K6663 2001
746.44'3041–dc21

2001020114

10 9 8 7 6 5 4 3 2 1

Published by Sterling Publishing Company, Inc.,
387 Park Avenue South, New York, NY 10016
© 2001 by Kooler Design Studio, Inc.
Distributed in Canada by Sterling Publishing
% Canadian Manda Group, One Atlantic Avenue, Suite 105
Toronto, Ontario, Canada M6K 3E7
Distributed in Great Britain and Europe by Cassell PLC
Wellington House, 125 Strand, London WC2R 0BB, England
Distributed in Australia by Capricorn Link (Australia) Pty Ltd.
P.O. Box 6651, Baulkham Hills, Business Centre, NSW 2153, Australia
All Rights Reserved

Sterling ISBN 0-8069-7188-6

If you have any questions or comments, please contact: Chapelle Ltd., Inc., P.O. Box 9252 Ogden, UT 84409 (801) 621-2777 • FAX (801) 621-2788 • e-mail: chapelle@ chapelleltd.com • website: www.chapelleltd.com

Table of Contents

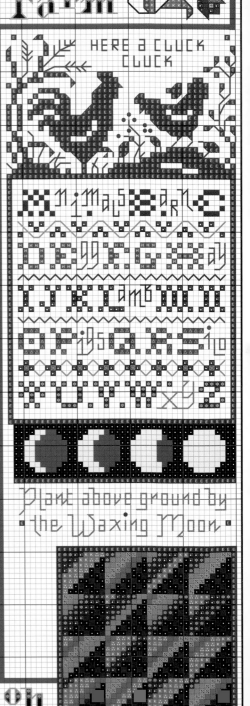

In an age when food is fast, bigger is better, consumption is conspicuous, and time would fly only if it slowed down, what better way to spend precious leisure time than to stitch a cheerful work of art? So we look time in the eye and laugh. The act of wrapping thread around thread allows us to become intimate with our creative selves while we lay the strands of our busy lives in order. We are released from clamoring time and refreshed by the simple enjoyment of working with our hands. The beauty we produce nourishes us both during creation and for years to come.

Samplers coaxed from these charts celebrate the bright colors of childhood. A joyful Noah's Ark reminds us of forty days of rain followed by an encouraging rainbow. Mistress Mary's garden blooms for us all year long, no matter how contrary she is, while the security of home, even if it is only a shoe, is celebrated with winsome images and comfortable sayings. And Old McDonald's farm is alive with creatures great and small—feathered, furred, and whimsical. Not only is our creative time fruitful but we can call back lighthearted youth with these joyous designs.

Adapting a portion of a design to even a tiny oasis of beauty the size of a handkerchief corner is all part of the versatility of counted-thread embroidery. Large work or small, our collection of 555 counted-thread cross-stitch designs is a wishing well to be dipped into again and again, for the lasting beauty of the works themselves as well as for the pleasure of a few tranquil moments.

I wish you pleasant stitching.

General Instructions

Introduction

Contained in this book are over 555 cross-stitch designs. Each double-page spread of graphed designs has its own color code. Each sampler's code is placed with the graphed sampler. To create one-of-a-kind motifs, vary colors in graphed designs.

Cross-stitch Items to Know

Fabric for Cross-stitch

Counted cross-stitch is worked on even-weave fabrics. These fabrics are manufactured specifically for counted-thread embroidery, and are woven with the same number of vertical as horizontal threads per inch.

Because the number of threads in the fabric is equal in each direction, each stitch will be the same size. The number of threads per inch in even-weave fabrics determines the size of a finished design.

Number of Strands

The number of strands used per stitch varies, depending on the fabric used. Generally, the rule to follow for cross-stitching is three strands on Aida 11, two strands on Aida 14, one or two strands on Aida 18 (depending on desired thickness of stitches), and one strand on Hardanger 22.

For backstitching, use one strand on all fabrics. When completing a French Knot (FK), use two strands and one wrap on all fabrics, unless otherwise directed.

Finished Design Size

To determine the size of the finished design, divide the stitch count by the number of threads per inch of fabric. When a design is stitched over two threads, divide stitch count by half the threads per inch. For example, if a design with a stitch count of 120 width and 250 height was stitched on a 28 count linen (over two threads making it 14 count), the finished size would be 8⅝" x 17⅞".

$$120 \div 14" = 8\tfrac{5}{8}" \text{ (width)}$$

$$250 \div 14" = 17\tfrac{7}{8}" \text{ (height)}$$

$$\text{Finished size} = 8\tfrac{5}{8}" \times 17\tfrac{7}{8}"$$

Preparing Fabric

Cut fabric at least 3" larger on all sides than the finished design size to ensure enough space for desired assembly. To prevent fraying, whipstitch or machine-zigzag along the raw edges or apply liquid fray preventive.

Needles for Cross-stitch

Blunt needles should slip easily through the fabric holes without piercing fabric threads. For fabric with 11 or fewer threads per inch, use a tapestry needle #24; for 14 threads per inch, use a tapestry needle #24, #26, or #28; for 18 or more threads per inch, use a tapestry needle #26 or #28. Avoid leaving the needle in the design area of the fabric. It may leave rust or a permanent impression on the fabric.

Floss

All numbers and color names on the codes represent the DMC brand of floss. Use 18" lengths of floss. For best coverage, separate the strands and dampen with a wet sponge, then put together the number of strands required for the fabric used.

Centering Design on Fabric

Fold the fabric in half horizontally, then vertically. Place a pin in the intersection to mark the center. Locate the center of the design on the graph. Begin stitching all designs at the center point of the graph and fabric.

Securing Floss

Insert needle up from the underside of the fabric at starting point. Hold 1" of thread behind the fabric and stitch over it, securing with the first few stitches. To finish thread, run under four or more stitches on the back of the design. Avoid knotting floss, unless working on clothing.

Another method of securing floss is the waste knot. Knot floss and insert needle down from the right top side of the fabric about 1" from design area. Work several stitches over the thread to secure. Cut off the knot later.

Carrying Floss

To carry floss, run floss under the previously worked stitches on the back. Do not carry thread across any fabric that is not or will not be stitched. Loose threads, especially dark ones, will show through the fabric.

Cleaning Finished Design

When stitching is finished, soak the fabric in cold water with a mild soap for five to ten minutes. Rinse well and roll in a towel to remove excess water. Do not wring. Place the piece face down on a dry towel and iron on a warm setting until the fabric is dry.

Stitching Techniques

Backstitch (BS)

1. Insert needle up between woven threads at A.

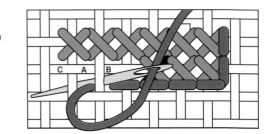

2. Go down at B, one opening to the right.

3. Come up at C.

4. Go down at A, one opening to the right.

Couching Thread Stitch (CT)

1. Complete a straight-stitch base by inserting needle up between woven threads at A. Go down at B. *Keep floss flat and loose.*

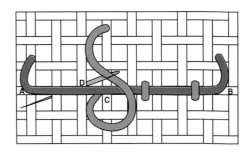

2. Make a short, tight straight stitch across floss base to "couch" straight stitch. Come up at C on one side of floss.

3. Go down at D on opposite side of floss. *This will cause floss to gather and pucker.*

Cross-stitch (XS)

Stitches are done in a row or, if necessary, one at a time in an area.

1. Insert needle up between woven threads at A.

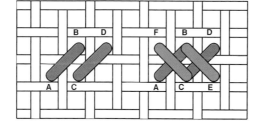

2. Go down at B , the opening diagonally across from A.

3. Come up at C and go down at D, etc.

4. To complete the top stitches creating an "X", come up at E and go down at B, come up at C and go down at F, etc. All top stitches should lie in the same direction.

French Knot (FK)

1. Insert needle up between woven threads at A, using one strand of embroidery floss.

2. Loosely wrap floss once around needle.

3. Go down at B, the opening across from A. Pull floss taut as needle is pushed down through fabric.

4. Carry floss across back of work between knots.

Lazy Daisy (LD)

1. Insert needle up between woven threads at A.

2. Go down at B, using same opening as A.

3. Come up at C, crossing under two threads. Pull through, holding floss under needle to form loop.

4. Go down at D, crossing one thread.

Long Stitch (LS)

1. Insert needle up between woven threads at A.

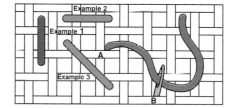

2. Go down at B, crossing two threads. Pull flat.

3. Repeat Steps 1–2 for each stitch. Stitch may be horizontal, vertical, or diagonal as indicated in Examples 1, 2, and 3. The length of the stitch should be the same as the length indicated on the graph.

eeh-eye-eeh-eye-oh

and on his farm
he had a cow

eeh-eye-eeh-eye-oh

Old
McDonald's
Farm

eeh-eye-eeh-eye-oh

and on his farm
he had a pig

eeh-eye-eeh-eye-oh

Old McDonald's Farm Sampler

DMC Floss	XS	BS	FK	LD
White	·			
677	☐		○	
676	+			
729	■			
945	■			
3854	▨			
3853	■			
3326	■			
3833	▨			
3832	△	⌐	●	
3831	❋	⌐		
815	■			
3609	◎			
3608	■			
3607	▣	⌐		
519	■			
794	▨			
793	■			
3807	E	⌐	●	
792	★	⌐		
3348	■			
989	N			
3346	■	⌐		O
562	K			
561	✛	⌐	●	
435	H	⌐		
3864 } 3863	■			
3862	■	⌐	●	
415	■			
451	▣		●	
535	■	⌐		
310	■	⌐		

DMC Floss

	XS	BS	FK	LD
White	·			
677	☐		○	
676	⊞			
729	■			
945	■			
3854	▨			
3853	■			
3326	■			
3833	◪			
3832	△	⌐_	●	
3831	❋	⌐_		
815	■	⌐_		
3609	⌂			
3608	■			
3607	▣	⌐_		
519	■			
794	⊡			
793	■			
3807	E	⌐_	●	
792	★	⌐_		
3348	■			
989	N			
3346	■	⌐_		⊘
562	K			
561	✛	⌐_	●	
435	H	⌐_		
3864 } 3863	■			
3862	■	⌐_	●	
415	■			
451	⊡		●	
535	■	⌐_		
310	▪	⌐_		

Bottom Left

Bottom Center

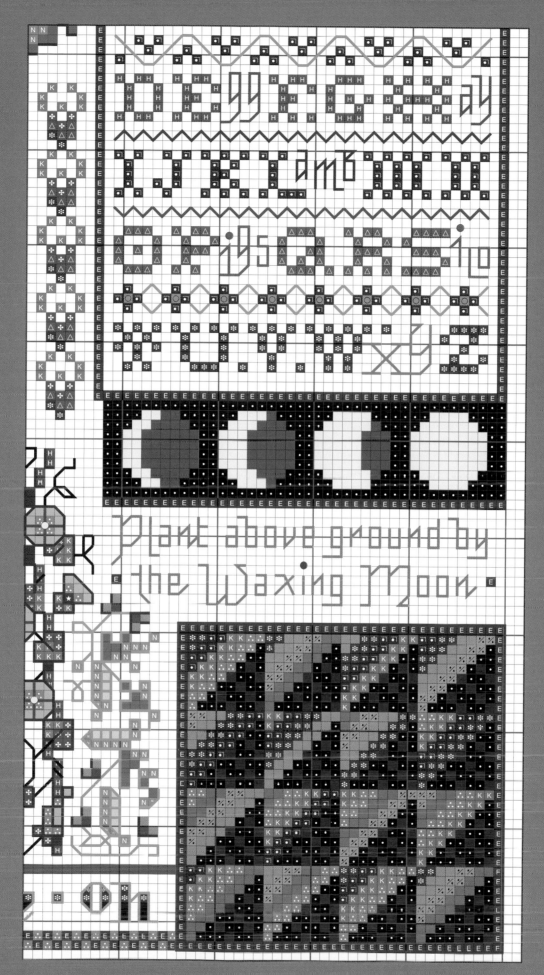

Plant above ground by the Waxing Moon

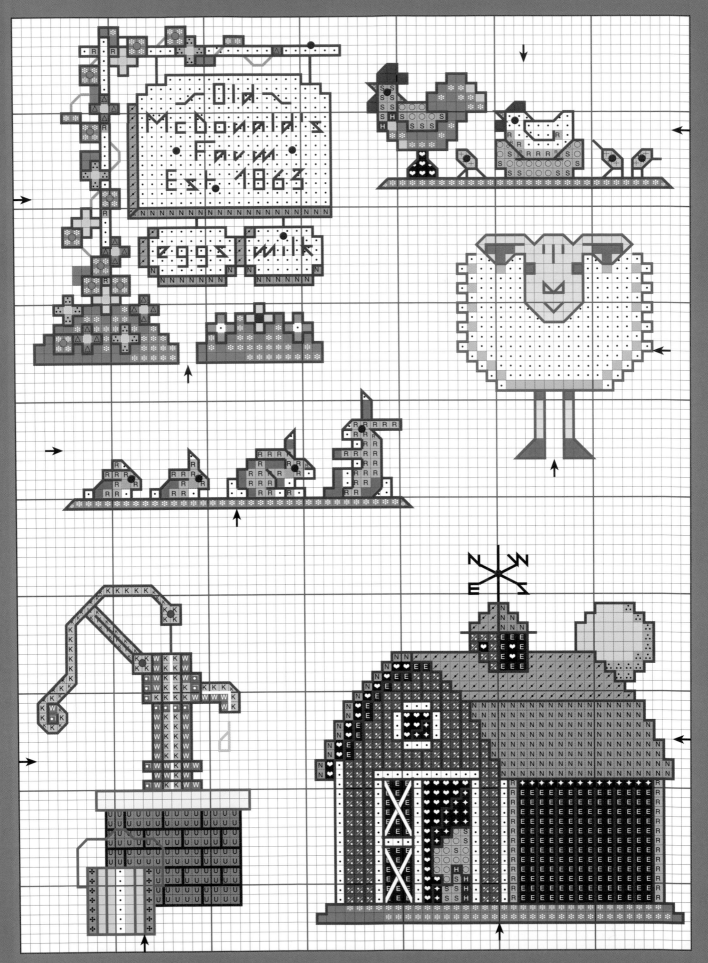

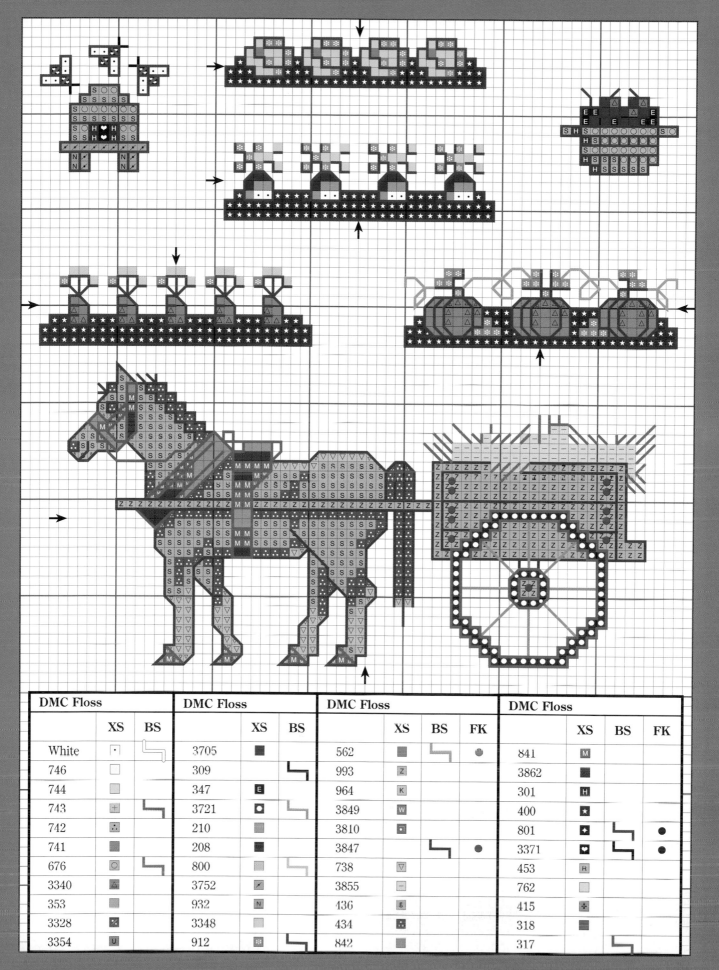

DMC Floss			DMC Floss			DMC Floss				DMC Floss			
	XS	BS		XS	BS		XS	BS	FK		XS	BS	FK
White	·		3705			562				841	M		
746			309			993	Z			3862			
744			347	E		964	K			301	H		
743	+		3721	O		3849	W			400	★		
742			210			3810				801	✚		●
741			208			3847			●	3371	♥		●
676	O		800			738	▽			453	R		
3340	△		3752	✎		3855	–			762			
353			932	N		436	ε			415	✿		
3328			3348			434				318			
3354	U		912			842				317			

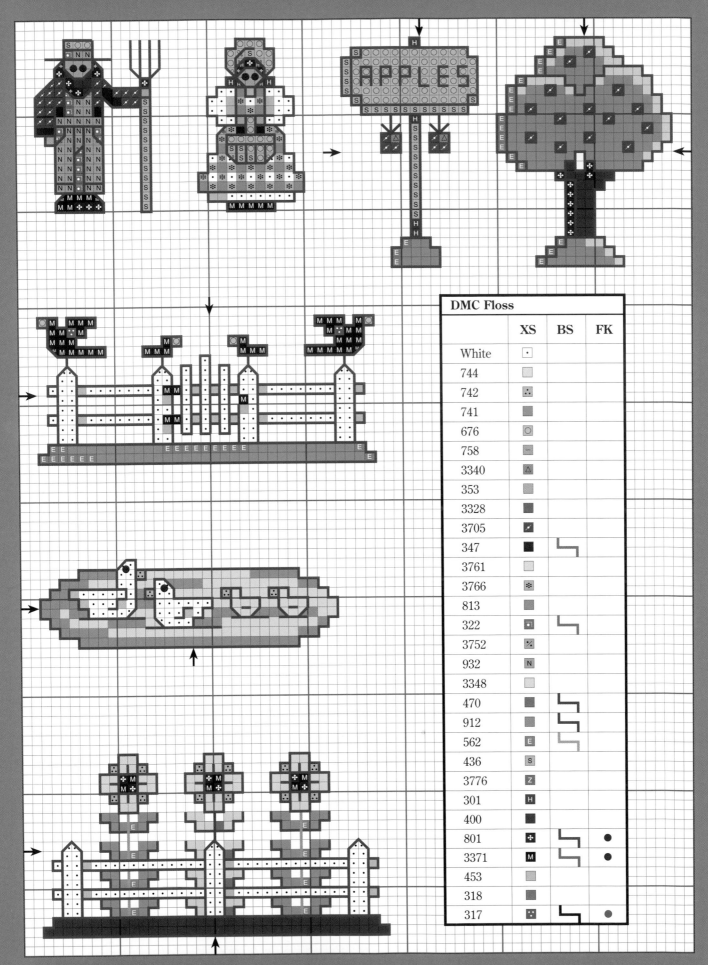

DMC Floss			
	XS	BS	FK
White	·		
744			
742			
741			
676	○		
758	–		
3340	△		
353			
3328			
3705			
347		⌐	
3761			
3766	❋		
813			
322	▣	⌐	
3752	⊠		
932	N		
3348			
470		⌐	
912		⌐	
562	E	⌐	
436	S		
3776	Z		
301	H		
400			
801	✛	⌐	●
3371	M	⌐	●
453			
318			
317	▣	⌐	●

18

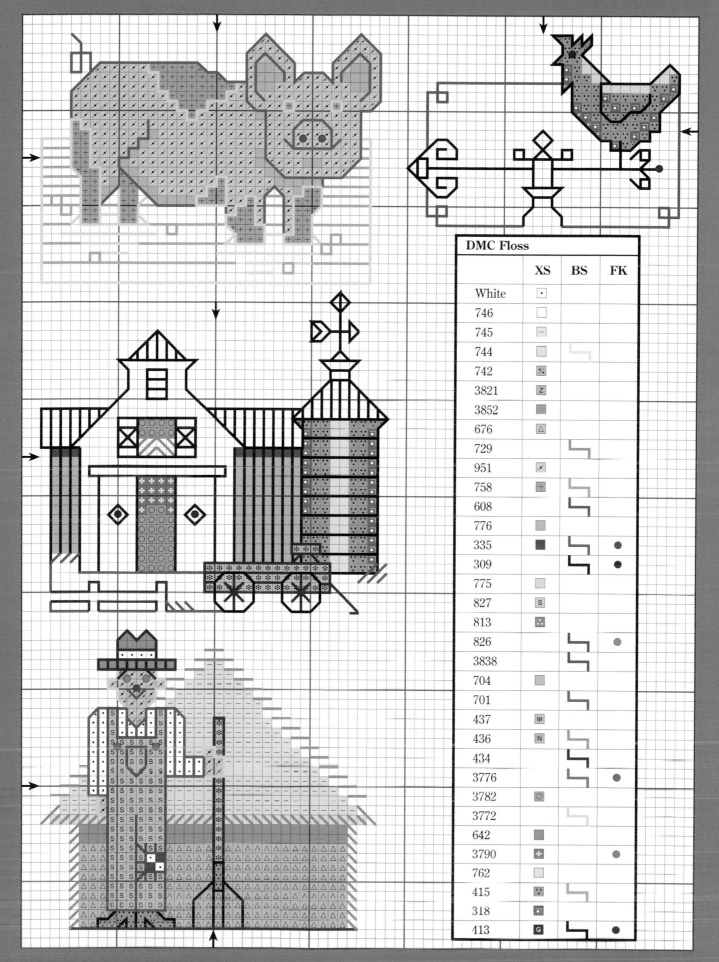

DMC Floss			
	XS	BS	FK
White	·		
746	☐		
745	▬		
744	☐		
742	⦂		
3821	Z		
3852	◼		
676	△		
729			
951	◢		
758	+		
608			
776	◼		
335	◼		●
309			●
775	☐		
827	S		
813	⦂		
826			●
3838			
704	◼		
701			
437	✳		
436	N		
434			
3776			●
3782	◙		
3772			
642	◼		
3790	⊞		●
762	☐		
415	⦂		
318	◘		
413	◙		●

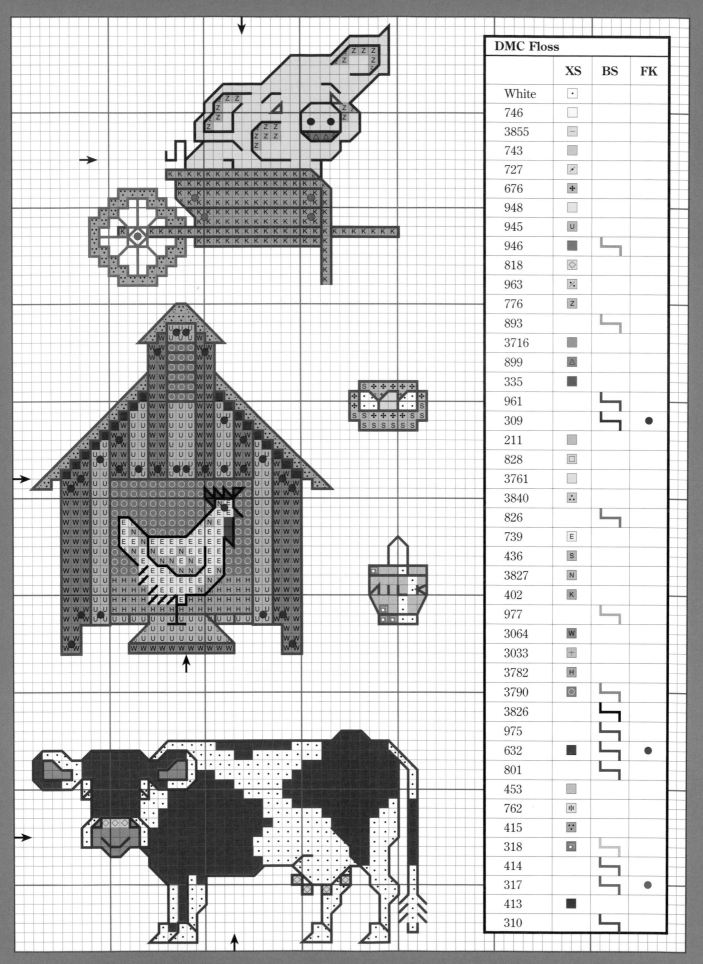

DMC Floss			
	XS	BS	FK
White	·		
746			
3855	−		
743			
727	◪		
676	✚		
948			
945	U		
946	■	⌐	
818	◇		
963	⁒		
776	Z		
893		⌐	
3716	■		
899	△		
335	■		
961		⌐	
309		⌐	●
211	▦		
828	□		
3761			
3840	⸬		
826		⌐	
739	E		
436	S		
3827	N		
402	K		
977		⌐	
3064	W		
3033	✚		
3782	H		
3790	◎	⌐	
3826		⌐	
975		⌐	
632	■	⌐	●
801		⌐	
453			
762	✳		
415	⸭		
318	▣	⌐	
414		⌐	
317		⌐	●
413	■		
310		⌐	

Mary
Mary
Quite
Contrary

How does your garden grow?

Mary, Mary, Quite Contrary Sampler

DMC Floss	XS	BS	CT
White	·		⊣⊢
3047	▨		
745	▢		
726	+		
3770	−		
945	▨		
741	■		
947	⦂		
900	❄		
606	■		
353	✕		
352	■		
351	◯		
3708	△		
956	N		
666	E	⌐	
815	W	⌐	
3609	▨		
3607	Z		
718	■		
915	✚	⌐	
210	▨		
553	■		
550	M	⌐	
341	▨		
340	S	⌐	
3746	✦		
333	■		
792		⌐	
827	U		
826	⦂	⌐	
824	◧		
311		⌐	

DMC Floss	XS	BS	LS	CT
747	▢			
959	■			
958	H			
3813	▽		╲	
3816	K			
3815	◙			⊣⊢
907	◇			⊣⊢
906	G	⌐		
936		⌐		
772	▢			
989	■		╲	
987	R			
986	■	⌐		
3013	▨			
370	♥			
890		⌐		
739	▢			
436	▨			
3827	B			
976	↔			
301	■	⌐		
300		⌐		
3790	✱			
3782	▨			
3024	J			
642	◕			
640	■			
415	▨			
414	★			
413	■			
3799		⌐		
310	▪	⌐		

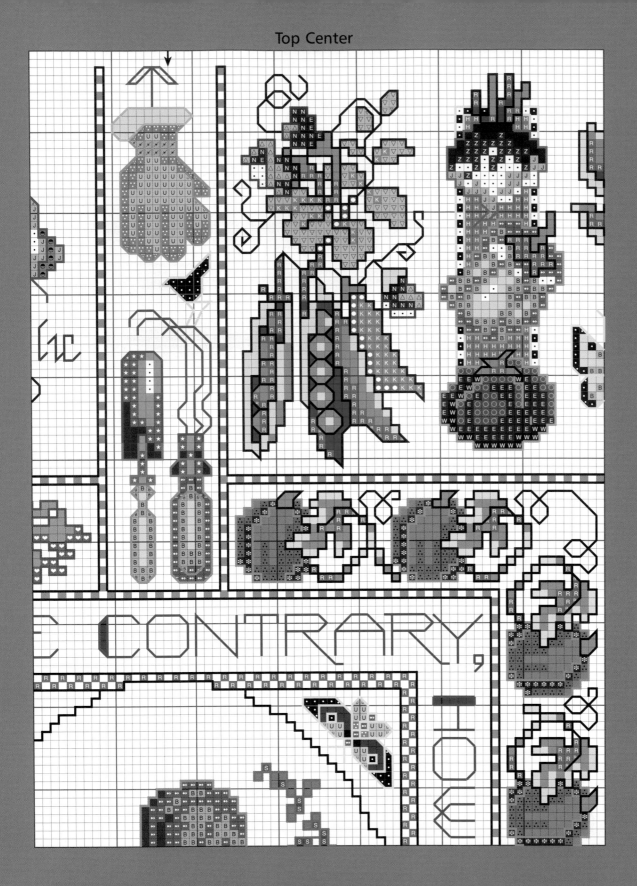

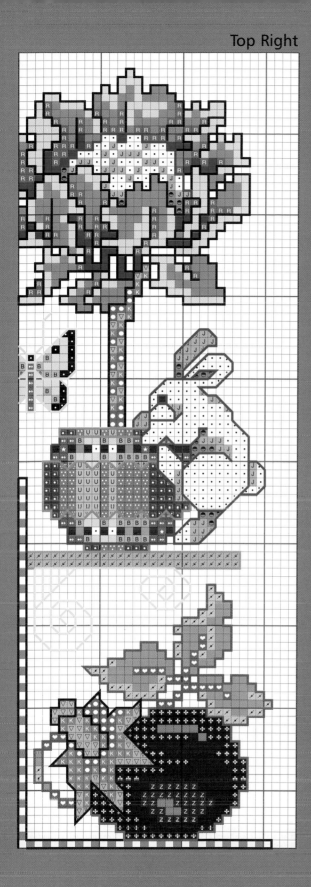

DMC Floss				DMC Floss				
	XS	BS	CT		XS	BS	LS	CT
White	·		⊣⊢	747				
3047				959				
745				958	H			
726	+			3813	▽		/	
3770	−			3816	K			
945				3815	◘			⊣⊢
741				907	◈			⊣⊢
947				906	G	⌐		
900	✳			936		⌐		
606	■			772				
353	✕			989			/	
352				987	R			
351	◎			986	■	⌐		
3708	△			3013				
956	N			370	♥			
666	E	⌐		890		⌐		
815	W	⌐		739	□			
3609				436	✎			
3607	Z			3827	B			
718	■			976	↔			
915	✚	⌐		301	■	⌐		
210	▨			300		⌐		
553	■			3790	✳			
550	M	⌐		3782				
341				3024	J			
340	S	⌐		642	◔			
3746	✦			640				
333	■			415				
792		⌐		414	✧			
827	U			413	■			
826	⋮			3799		⌐		
824	◧			310	■			
311		⌐						

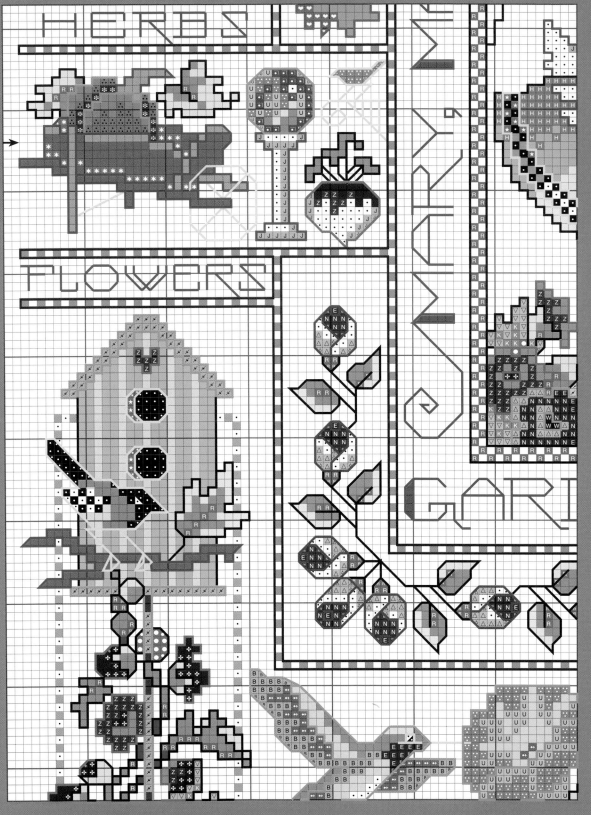

DMC Floss	XS	BS	CT
White	·		⊣⊢
3047	◢		
745	▢		
726	+		
3770	–		
945	▢		
741	▪		
947	⁙		
900	✳		
606	▪		
353	×		
352	▪		
351	○		
3708	△		
956	N		
666	E	⌐	
815	W	⌐	
3609	▪		
3607	Z		
718	▪		
915	✚	⌐	
210	⁒	⌐	
553	▪		
550	M	⌐	
341	▪		
340	S	⌐	
3746	◆		
333	▪		
792		⌐	
827	U		
826	⁙	⌐	
824	▪		
311		⌐	

DMC Floss	XS	BS	LS	CT
747	▢			
959	▪			
958	H			
3813	▽		╲	
3816	K			
3815	◨			⊣⊢
907	◇			⊣⊢
906	G	⌐		
936	▪	⌐		
772	▢			
989	▪		╲	
987	R			
986	▪	⌐		
3013	▪			
370	♥	⌐		
890	▪	⌐		
739	▢			
436	◢			
3827	B			
976	▸▸			
301	▪	⌐		
300		⌐		
3790	✳			
3782	▪			
3024	J			
642	◕			
640	▪			
415	▪			
414	★			
413	▪			
3799		⌐		
310	▪			⌐

Bottom Left

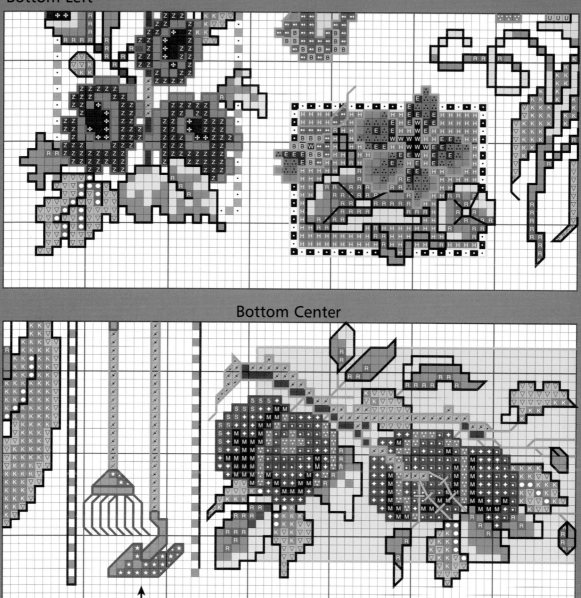

Bottom Center

Bottom Right

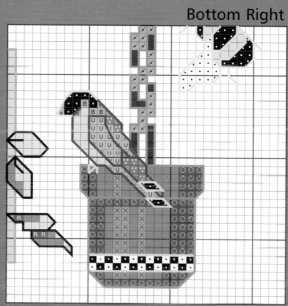

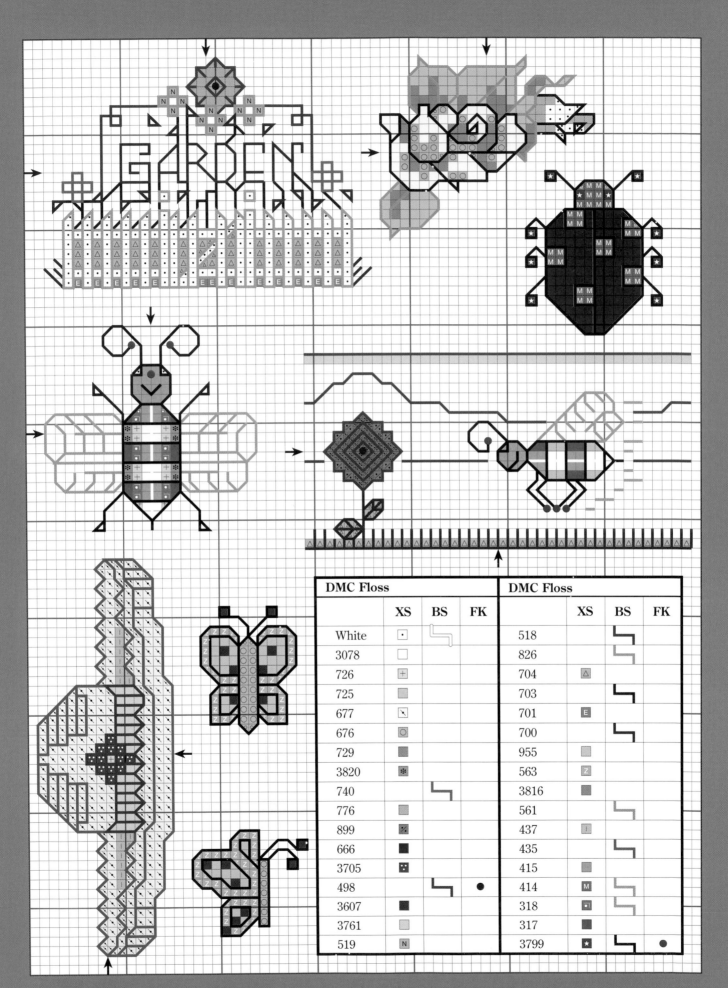

DMC Floss	XS	BS	FK	DMC Floss	XS	BS	FK
White	·			518			
3078	□			826			
726	+			704	△		
725	■			703			
677	◤			701	E		
676	○			700			
729	■			955	■		
3820	✳			563	Z		
740				3816	■		
776	■			561			
899	▨			437	I		
666	■			435			
3705	▨			415	■		
498			●	414	M		
3607	■			318	▣		
3761	■			317	■		
519	N			3799	★		●

DMC Floss			DMC Floss			
	XS	BS		XS	BS	FK
White	·		561			
Ecru	−		955			
3046			993	N		
3821	+		3815			
309			3814			
800			937			
794			436			
931			400			●
3807			838			
564			801			
563			318			

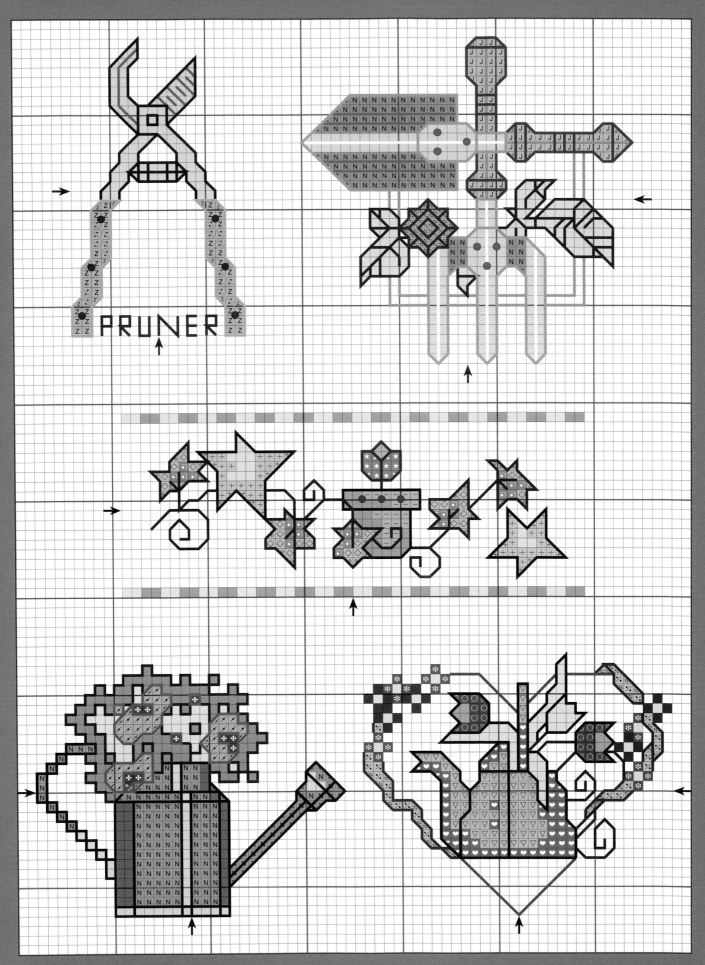

PRUNER

DMC Floss			
	XS	BS	FK
White	·		
745			
743	+		
676	△		
729			
948			
754	−		
758			
3801	❋		
666	■		
605			
3608	○		
3607	■		
718			
211	✎		
554	F		
553	✚		
327			
800			
3840	⦂		
794	A		
3838			
772			
989	M		
955	⦂		
913			
3813	◇		
501			
3817	▽		
3816	▣		
3815	♥		
437	J		
3856	⦂		
402	▣		
301			●
3854	H		
3853	G		
3827	Z		
3826	■		
356			●
762			
415	N		
318	W		●
414			
535			●

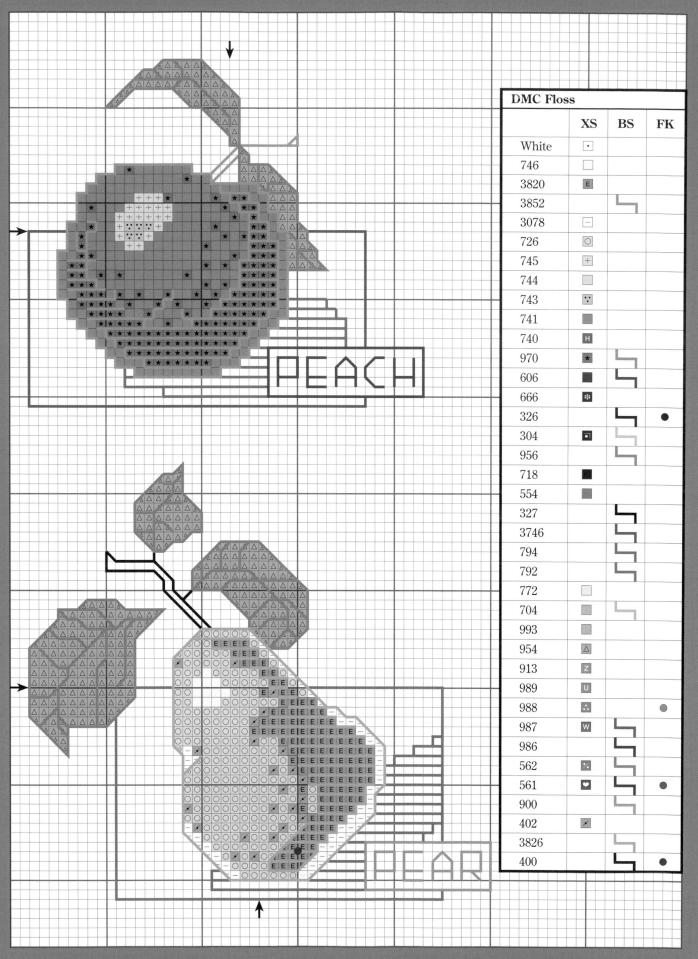

DMC Floss			
	XS	**BS**	**FK**
White	·		
746	☐		
3820	E		
3852		⌐	
3078	−		
726	○		
745	+		
744	▨		
743	⁙		
741	▨		
740	H		
970	★	⌐	
606	▨	⌐	
666	❊		
326		⌐	●
304	▣	⌐	
956		⌐	
718	▨		
554	▨		
327		⌐	
3746		⌐	
794		⌐	
792		⌐	
772	☐		
704	▨		
993	▨		
954	△		
913	Z		
989	U		
988	⁙		●
987	W	⌐	
986		⌐	
562	﹪	⌐	
561	♥	⌐	●
900			
402	⁄		
3826		⌐	
400		⌐	●

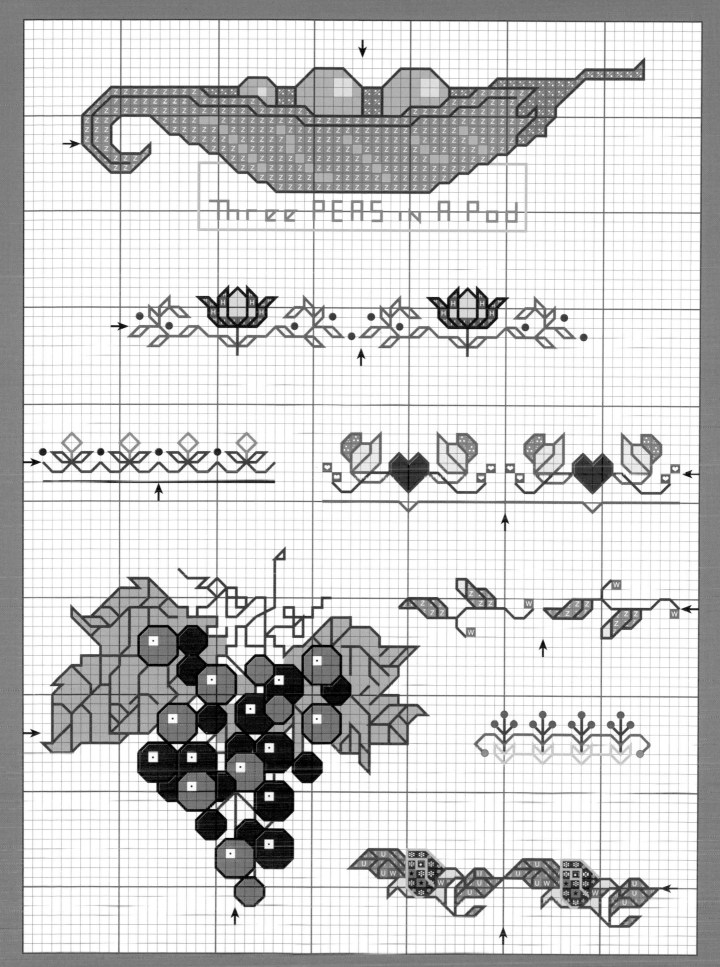

Three PEAS in A Pod

DMC Floss			
	XS	**BS**	**FK**
White	·	⌐	
3823	▢		
727	▢		
3820		⌐	●
741	▪	⌐	
606		⌐	●
3713	▢		
3708	◿		
963	−		
3716	▪		
957	◉		
899	⦂		
961	E		
326	■	⌐	●
3608	▨		
828	+		
827	▢		
775	✕		
334	▪		
312	✳	⌐	
800	⁖		
809	✜	⌐	
798		⌐	
747	▢		
3766	z		
807		⌐	●
517		⌐	
772	▢		
704	H		
954	▪		
989	⊡		
987	▪		
986		⌐	
561	★		
3827	▪		
738	△		
436	N		
434		⌐	●
414		⌐	●
317		⌐	
452	▪		
451	K		
535		⌐	●

Sunflower
angel

DMC Floss			
	XS	BS	FK
White	·		
3823			
727	+		
744			
743	▽		
742	✖		
3855	—		
3854			
3821	Z		
729		⌐	
948			
761			
350		⌐	
606	◉		
3607			
208		⌐	●
3756			
800	⫽		
827	E	⌐	
3325			
813	⫶		
334	★		
322		⌐	
312			
772			
704		⌐	
955	U		
913	N		
563	⊡		
562		⌐	
561	✚		
989	⫶		
987			
986	W	⌐	
842			
841	‖		
3776	△		
976	S		
975	✳	⌐	●
301		⌐	
3799		⌐	●
310	▪	⌐	

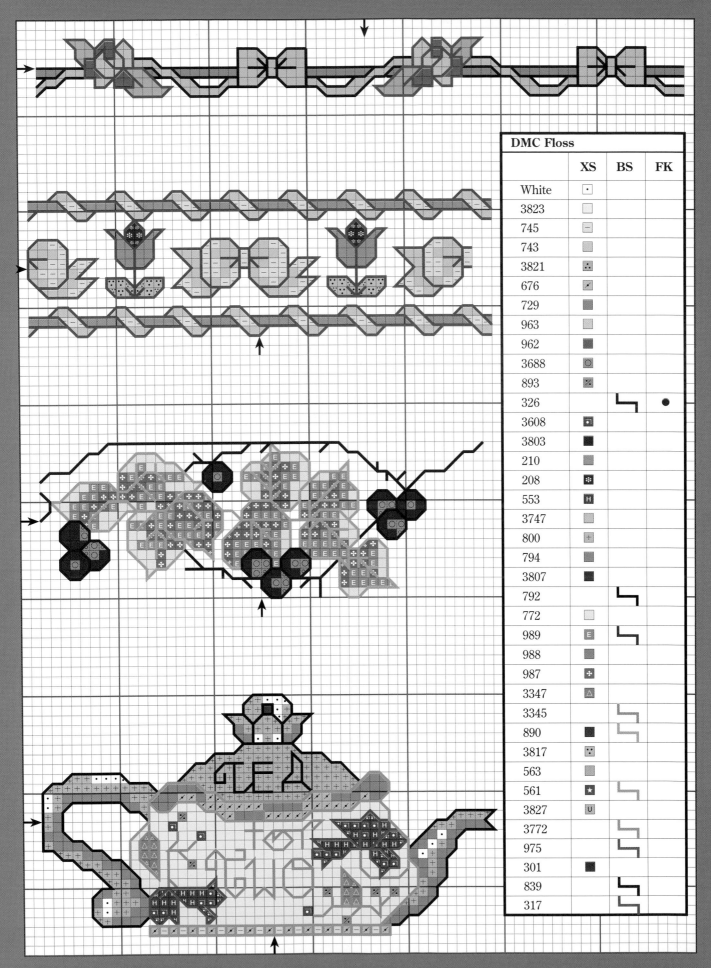

DMC Floss			
	XS	**BS**	**FK**
White	·		
3823			
745	−		
743			
3821	∴		
676	◢		
729			
963			
962			
3688	○		
893	▨		
326		⌐	●
3608	▣		
3803	■		
210			
208	❋		
553	H		
3747			
800	+		
794			
3807	■	⌐	
792		⌐	
772			
989	E	⌐	
988			
987	✛		
3347	△		
3345		⌐	
890	■	⌐	
3817	∴		
563			
561	★	⌐	
3827	U		
3772		⌐	
975		⌐	
301	■		
839		⌐	
317		⌐	

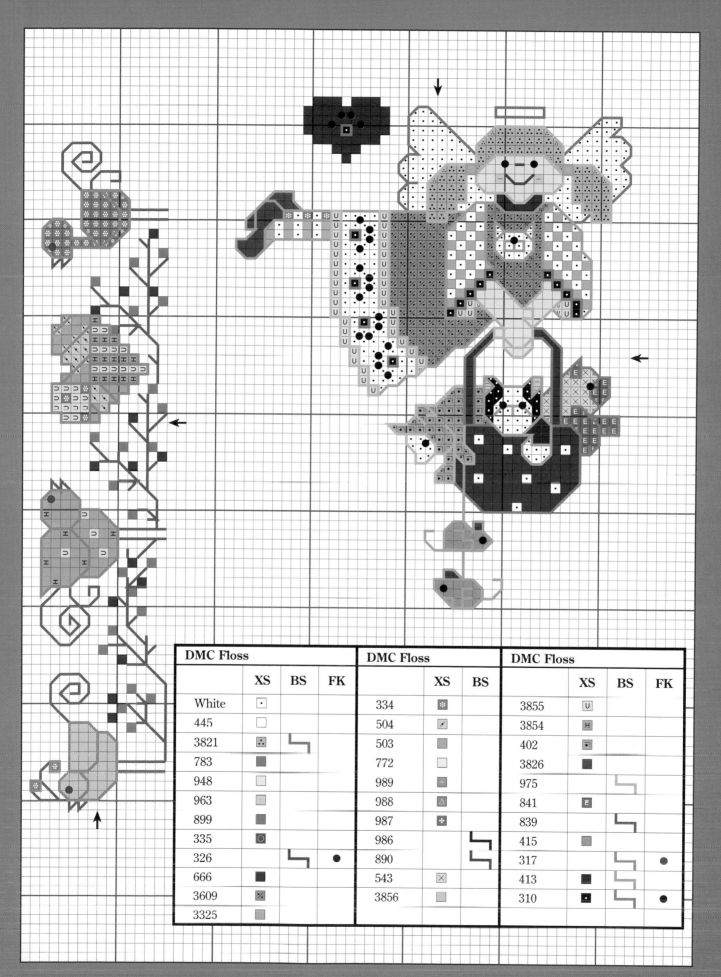

DMC Floss	XS	BS	FK
White	·		
445			
3821	⠿	⌐	
783	■		
948			
963			
899	■		
335	◎		
326		⌐	●
666	■		
3609	⊠		
3325			

DMC Floss	XS	BS
334	✳	
504	╱	
503		
772		
989	✚	
988	△	
987	✚	
986		⌐
890		⌐
543	⊠	
3856		

DMC Floss	XS	BS	FK
3855	U		
3854	H		
402	⊡		
3826	■		
975		⌐	
841	E		
839		⌐	
415	■		
317		⌐	●
413	■	⌐	
310	⊡	⌐	●

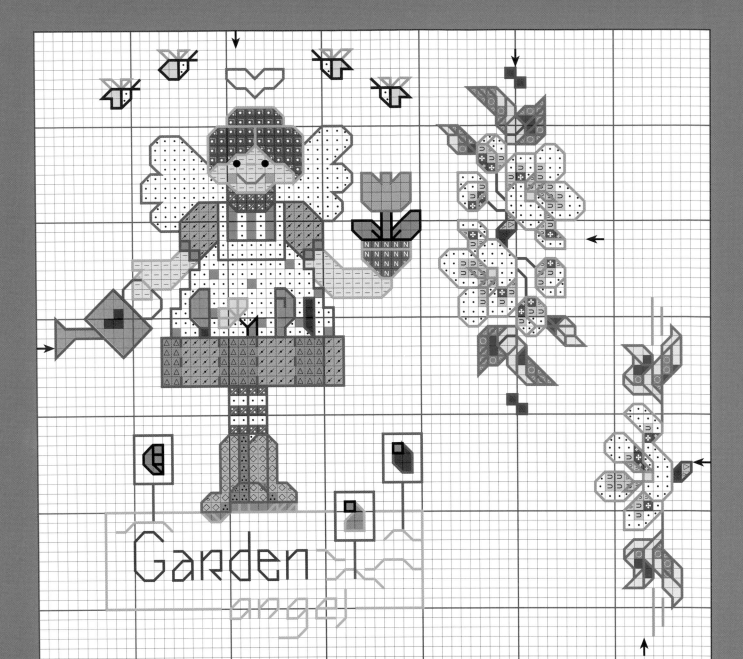

DMC Floss			DMC Floss			DMC Floss			DMC Floss			
	XS	BS		XS	BS		XS	BS		XS	BS	FK
White	·		962	E		792	■	⌐	738	Z		
712			335	✚		3761			436	⋮		
744			326		⌐	597	■	⌐	3776	N		
741	■		3609	■		3817	◈		3864	▽		
729	■	⌐	3607	■		502	⋮		3862	■		
948	−		3685	★	⌐	501	■	⌐	3772	◧		
761	■		209	⁒		772			433		⌐	
353	◹		208	H		989	■		801		⌐	
352	△		550	◕	⌐	988	◉	⌐	415	■		
350	■	⌐	775	＋		987	✳	⌐	413		⌐	
819	⊠		334		⌐	986	■	⌐	310		⌐	●
963	U		931		⌐	3345		⌐				

BLOOM WHERE YOU'RE PLANTED

RICH man

Beggerman
Thief
Doctor
Lawyer
Merchant
Chief

poor MAN

Rich Man, Poor Man, Sampler

DMC Floss	XS	BS	FK	DMC Floss	XS	BS	FK
White	·			825	▪	⌐	
3078	☐			3811	J		
3855	+			964	R		
676	◻			958	✛	⌐	
725	✎			704	☐		
3852	S			703	✎		
780	✳	⌐		955	◻		
948	☐			954	✕		
945	¬			912	G		
754	◻			562	◗		
758	⁙			561	■	⌐	
971	◎			739	▽		
947	W			738	K		
963	◇			436	↔		
352	⁒			3827	B		
957	N			977	♥		
956	■			3776	■	⌐	
606	❊	⌐	●	3773	F		
321	⁜	⌐		3772	Z		
816	■	⌐		3858	▲	⌐	
3608	U	⌐	●	841	■		
211	▦			840	✦	⌐	
210	Z			839	■	⌐	
208	■	⌐		762	☐		
340	M			415	A		
775	☐			318	E		
3841	H			317	★		●
799	■			413	■	⌐	
826	△	⌐		310	▪	⌐	●

DMC Floss	XS	BS	FK	DMC Floss	XS	BS	FK
White	·			825	▣	⌐	
3078	☐			3811	J		
3855	+			964	R		
676	▢			958	✚	⌐	
725	◢			704	▢		
3852	S			703	◢		
780	✹	⌐		955	▢		
948	☐			954	✕		
945	▬			912	G		
754	▢			562	◉		
758	⦂			561	▪	⌐	
971	◎			739	▽		
947	W			738	K		
963	◇			436	↔		
352	◪			3827	B		
957	N			977	♥		
956	▪			3776	▪	⌐	
606	✸	⌐	●	3773	F		
321	⦂	⌐		3772	7		
816	▪	⌐		3858	▲	⌐	
3608	U	⌐	●	841	▪		
211	▪			840	✦		
210	Z			839	▪	⌐	
208	▪	⌐		762	☐		
340	M			415	A		
775	▢			318	E		
3841	H			317	★		●
799	▪			413	▪	⌐	
826	△	⌐		310	■	⌐	●

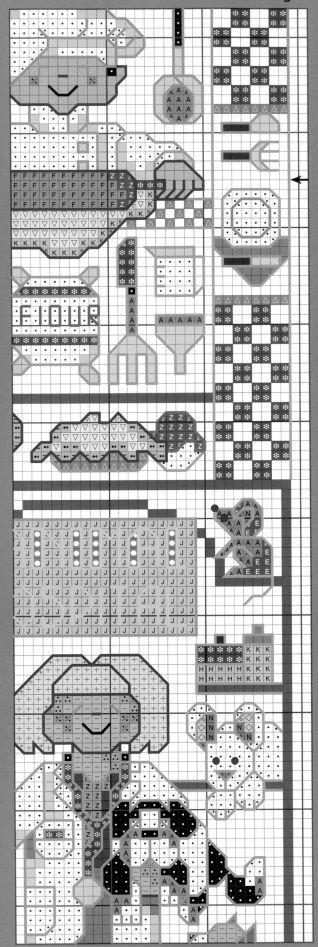

DMC Floss				DMC Floss			
	XS	BS	FK		XS	BS	FK
White	·			825	▣	⌐	
3078	▢			3811	J		
3855	+			964	R		
676	▣			958	✢	⌐	
725	✎			704	▢		
3852	S			703	✎		
780	✳	⌐		955	▣		
948	▢			954	✕		
945	−			912	G		
754	▣			562	◉		
758	⋰			561	■	⌐	
971	◯			739	▽		
947	W			738	K		
963	◇			436	••		
352	⅟			3827	B		
957	N			977	♥		
956	■			3776	▣	⌐	
606	✳	⌐	●	3773	F		
321	⋰	⌐		3772	Z		
816	■	⌐		3858	▲	⌐	
3608	U	⌐	●	841	■		
211	▣			840	✦		
210	Z			839	■	⌐	
208	■	⌐		762	▢		
340	M			415	A		
775	▢			318	E		
3841	H			317	★		●
799	■			413	■	⌐	
826	△	⌐		310	◼	⌐	●

Bottom Left

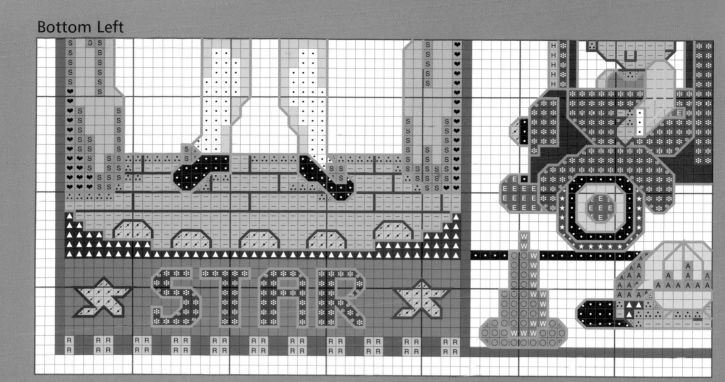

Bottom Center

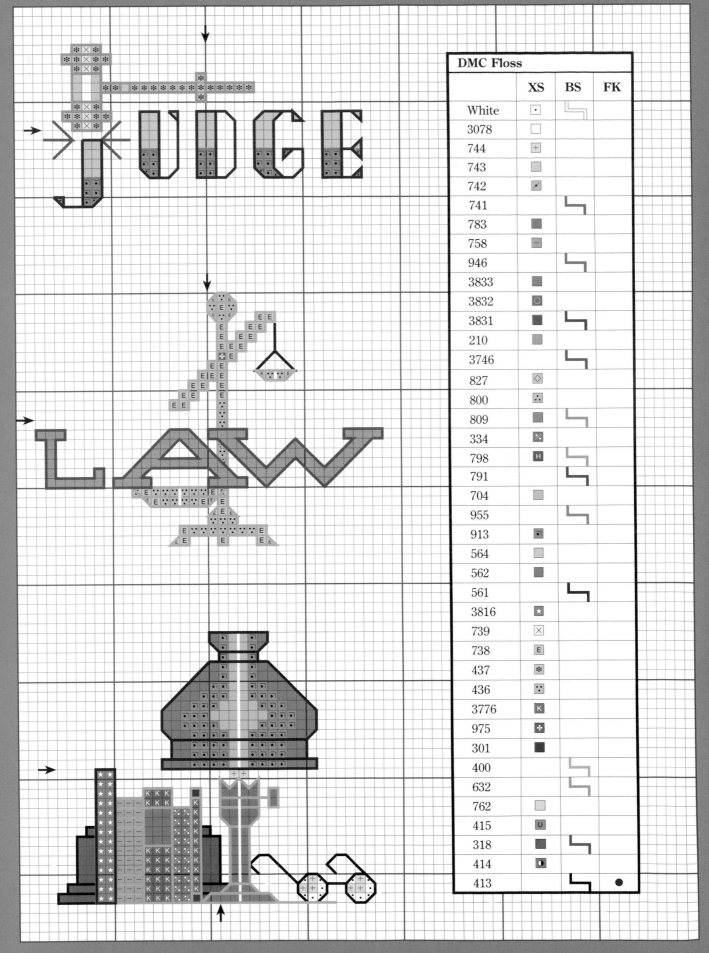

DMC Floss			
	XS	BS	FK
White	·		
3078			
744	+		
743			
742			
741			
783			
758	−		
946			
3833			
3832	⊙		
3831			
210			
3746			
827	◇		
800			
809			
334			
798	H		
791			
704			
955			
913			
564			
562			
561			
3816	★		
739	✕		
738	E		
437	✳		
436			
3776	K		
975			
301			
400			
632			
762			
415	U		
318			
414	◑		
413			●

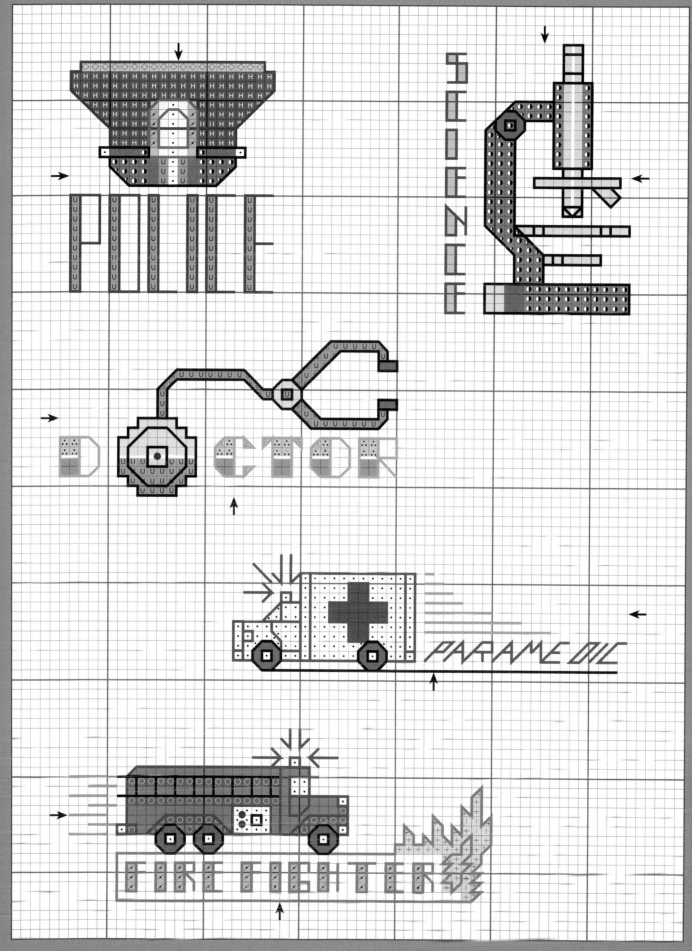

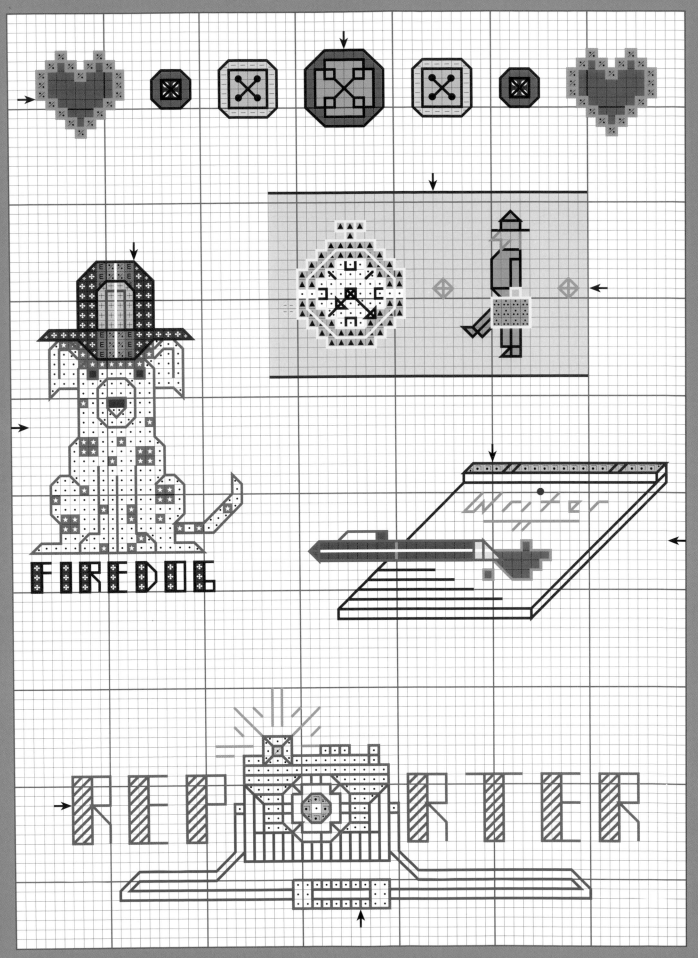

DMC Floss			
	XS	BS	FK
White	·		
3078	□		
727	−		
726	◸		
725			
3822	+		
676	▲		
729			
951			
971			
3708			
352	◯		
350	■		
817	⊡		
815			
3326	▨		
335			
3833	E		
3832	■		
3831	◨		●
3608	■		
917			
211			
209	■		
208	◻		●
800	⊡		
3325			
322	✳		●
798			
747			
959	H		
704			
954			
561	■		
738	U		
3855	☒		
3854	Z		
402	▨		
976			
301			
762			
415	■		
414	▲		
413	■		
535			●

67

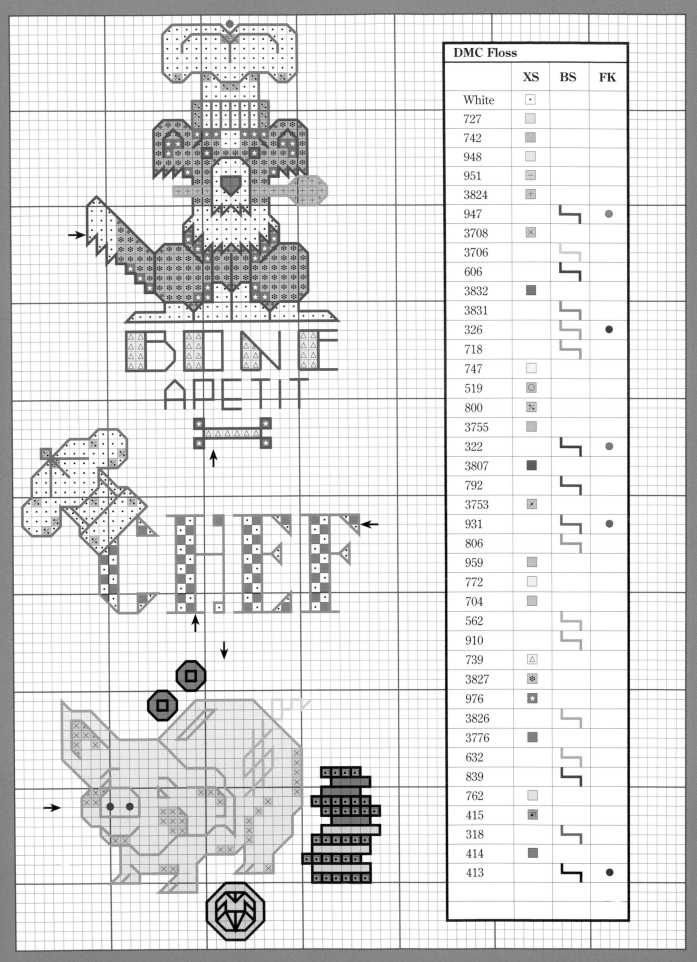

DMC Floss			
	XS	**BS**	**FK**
White	⊡		
727	▦		
742	▦		
948	▦		
951	⊟		
3824	⊞		
947		⌐	●
3708	⊠		
3706		⌐	
606		⌐	
3832	■		
3831		⌐	
326		⌐	●
718		⌐	
747	▢		
519	◎		
800	▨		
3755	▦		
322		⌐	●
3807	■		
792		⌐	
3753	◪		
931		⌐	●
806		⌐	
959	▦		
772	▢		
704	▦		
562		⌐	
910		⌐	
739	△		
3827	▣		
976	★		
3826		⌐	
3776	■		
632		⌐	
839		⌐	
762	▢		
415	⊡		
318		⌐	
414	▦		
413		⌐	●

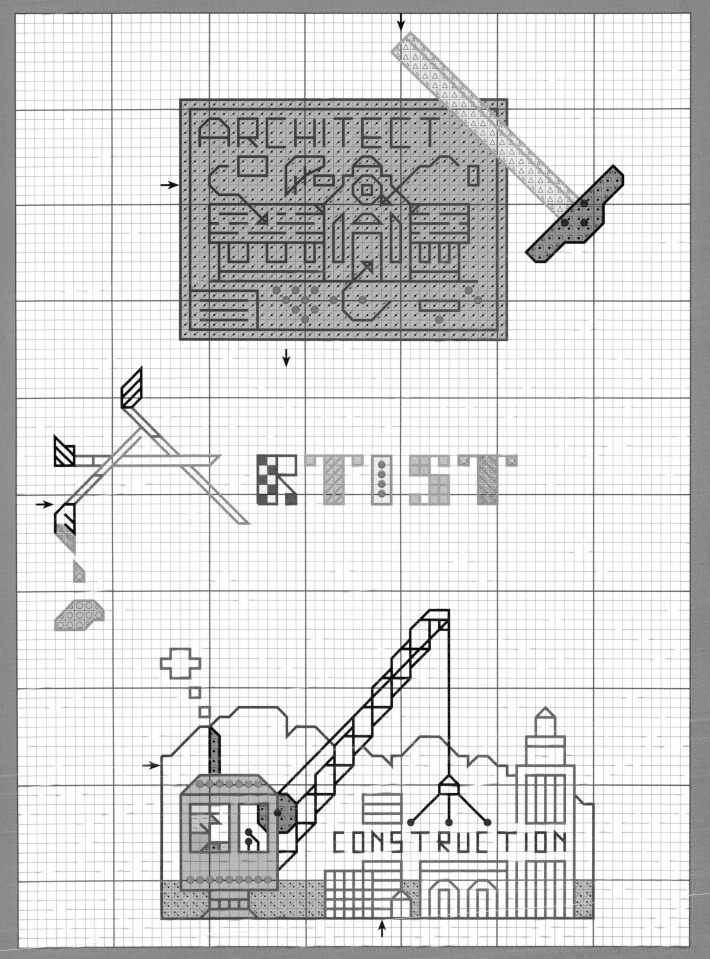

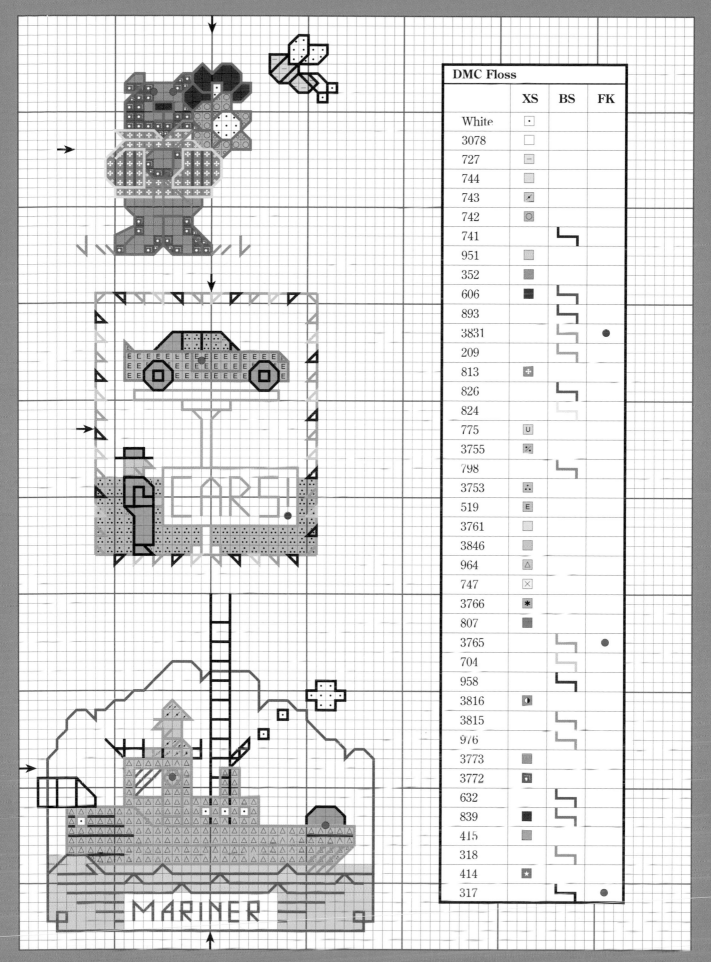

DMC Floss			
	XS	**BS**	**FK**
White	·		
3078			
727	−		
744			
743			
742	○		
741		⌐	
951			
352			
606		⌐	
893		⌐	
3831		⌐	●
209		⌐	
813	✛		
826		⌐	
824			
775	U		
3755			
798		⌐	
3753			
519	E		
3761			
3846			
964	△		
747	⊠		
3766	✳		
807			
3765		⌐	●
704		⌐	
958		⌐	
3816			
3815		⌐	
976		⌐	
3773			
3772			
632		⌐	
839		⌐	
415			
318		⌐	
414	✦		
317		⌐	●

The Old Woman

Who Lived in a Shoe

She had so many children she didn't know what to do.

Old Woman, Who Lived in a Shoe Sampler

DMC Floss	XS	BS	DMC Floss	XS	BS	FK
White	·		959	M		
3823	□		991		⌐	
745	–		954	▽		
744	○		912	◐		
676	▨		772	□		
948	□		989	K	⌐	
3855	✎		368	S		
3854	E		320	▨		
3825	▨		367	W	⌐	
722	✤		739	✎		
3713	+		738	↔		
3689	▨		437	□		
3832	▨		402	Z		
606	▣		3776	▨		
666	■		301	◖		
321	★		842	▨		
3608	▨		3863	N		
211	▨		3773	U		
210	⬡		3772	▨		
208	▨		3790	▨		
3756	✕		801	♥	⌐	●
775	▨		762	◇		
800	△		415	▨		
799	▨		414	H		
798	✳	⌐	413	■	⌐	◯
964	✴		310	▣	⌐	●

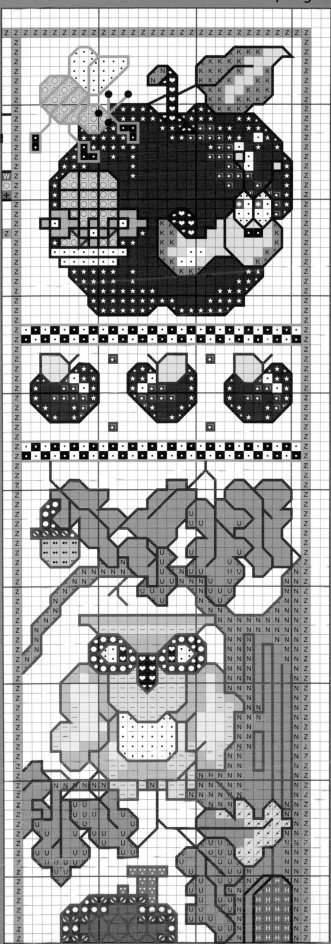

DMC Floss			DMC Floss			
	XS	BS		XS	BS	FK
White	⊡		959	M		
3823	☐		991		⌐	
745	−		954	▽		
744	◎		912	◐		
676	■		772	☐		
948	☐		989	K	⌐	
3855	⟋		368	S		
3854	E		320	■		
3825	■		367	W	⌐	
722	✚		739	⟋		
3713	＋		738	••		
3689	■		437	☐		
3832	％		402	Z		
606	◨		3776	■		
666	■		301	◖		
321	★		842	■		
3608	■		3863	N		
211	■		3773	U		
210	⁙		3772	■		
208	■		3790	▦		
3756	✕		801	♥	⌐	●
775	☐		762	◇		
800	△		415	■		
799	■		414	H		
798	✳	⌐	413	■	⌐	●
964	✴		310	◼	⌐	●

77

DMC Floss			DMC Floss			
	XS	**BS**		**XS**	**BS**	**FK**
White	·		959	M		
3823	▫		991		⌐	
745	−		954	▽		
744	○		912	◑		
676	▪		772	▫		
948	▪		989	K	⌐	
3855	✗		368	S		
3854	E		320	▪		
3825	▪		367	W	⌐	
722	✚		739	✗		
3713	+		738	▸▸		
3689	▪		437	□		
3832	▨		402	Z		
606	▣		3776	▪		
666	■		301	◖		
321	★		842	▪		
3608	■		3863	N		
211	▪		3773	U		
210	⠢		3772	■		
208	■		3790	⠢		
3756	⊠		801	♥	⌐	●
775	▪		762	◇		
800	△		415	▪		
799	▪		414	H		
798	✳	⌐	413	■	⌐	○
964	✺		310	▪	⌐	●

Bottom Left

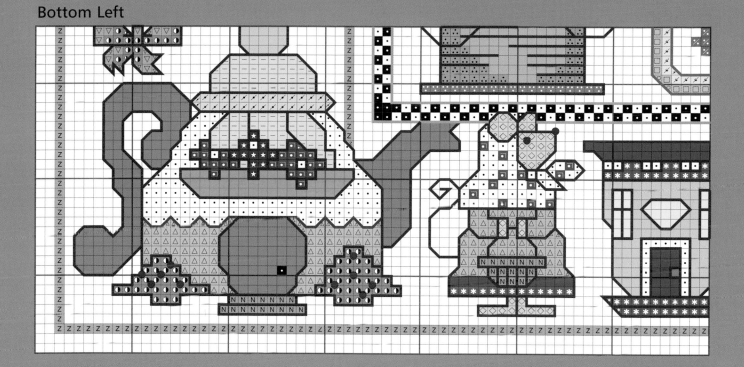

Bottom Center

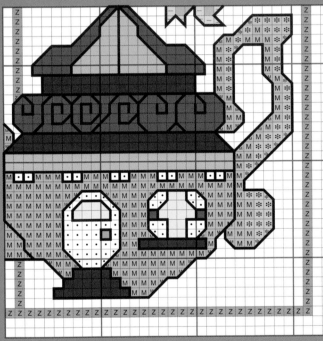

Bottom Right

DMC Floss			DMC Floss			
	XS	BS		XS	BS	FK
White	·		959	M		
3823	▫		991		⌐	
745	▬		954	▽		
744	⊙		912	◑		
676	▪		772	▫		
948	▪		989	K	⌐	
3855	✎		368	S		
3854	E		320	▪		
3825	▪		367	W	⌐	
722	✤		739	✎		
3713	+		738	↔		
3689	▪		437	▫		
3832	⁒		402	Z		
606	◙		3776	▪		
666	▪		301	◖		
321	★		842	▪		
3608	▪		3863	N		
211	▪		3773	U		
210	∴		3772	▪		
208	▪		3790	⊡		
3756	×		801	♥	⌐	●
775	▫		762	◇		
800	△		415	▪		
799	▪		414	H		
798	✴	⌐	413	▪	⌐	○
964	✳		310	◘	⌐	●

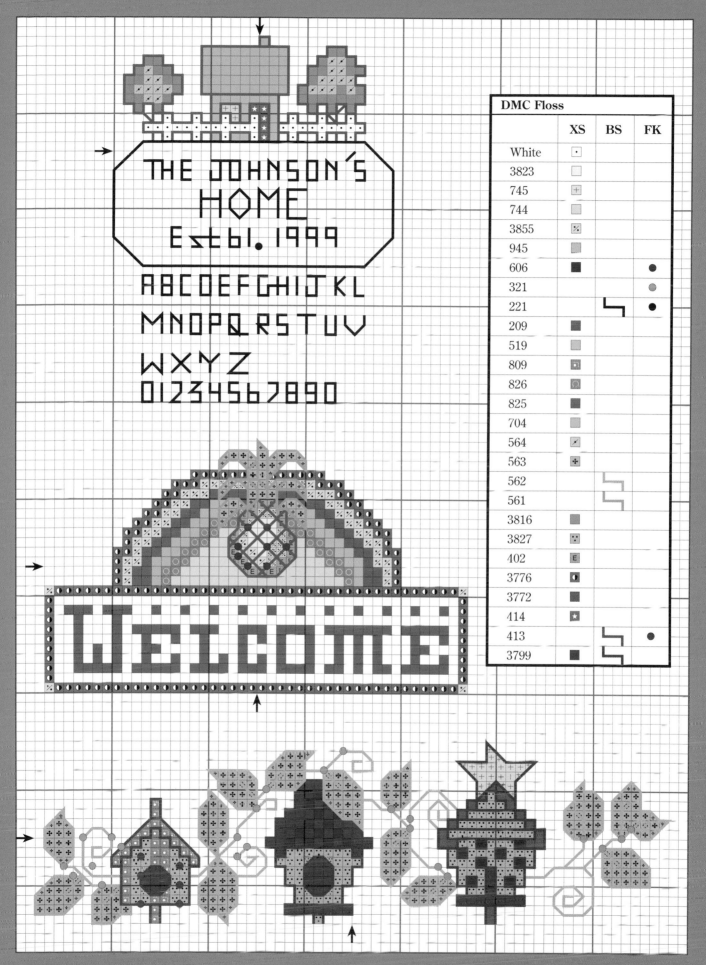

THE JOHNSON'S
HOME
Estbl. 1999

ABCDEFGHIJKL
MNOPQRSTUV
WXYZ
0123456789O

Welcome

DMC Floss			
	XS	BS	FK
White	·		
3823			
745	+		
744			
3855	⊘		
945			
606			●
321			●
221		⌐	●
209			
519			
809	⊡		
826	⊙		
825			
704			
564	⊠		
563	+		
562		⌐	
561		⌐	
3816			
3827	⋮		
402	E		
3776	◖		
3772			
414	★		
413		⌐	●
3799			

83

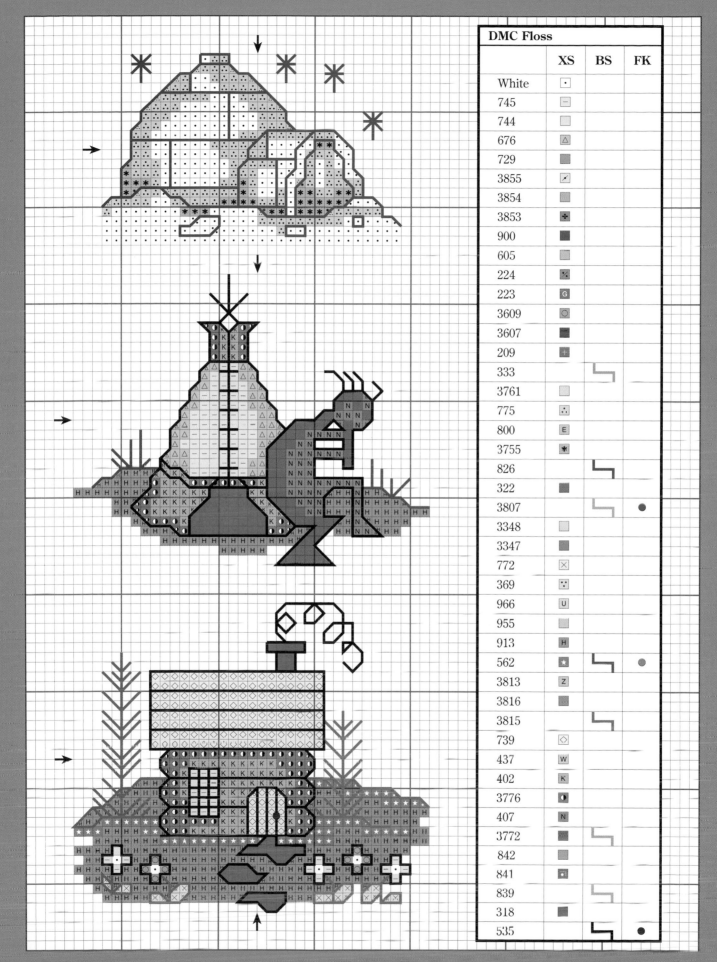

DMC Floss	XS	BS	FK
White	·		
745	−		
744	▢		
676	△		
729	▣		
3855	◪		
3854	▦		
3853	✚		
900	▪		
605	▨		
224	▨		
223	G		
3609	○		
3607	▦		
209	✚		
333		⌐	
3761	▢		
775	⠖		
800	E		
3755	✦		
826	▦	⌐	
322	▪		
3807		⌐	●
3348	▢		
3347	▦		
772	⨯		
369	⠖		
966	U		
955	▨		
913	H		
562	★	⌐	●
3813	Z		
3816	▦		
3815		⌐	
739	◇		
437	W		
402	K		
3776	◑		
407	N		
3772	▨	⌐	
842	▨		
841	▣		
839		⌐	
318	▪		
535		⌐	●

85

DMC Floss			DMC Floss			DMC Floss			DMC Floss			
	XS	FK		XS	BS		XS	BS		XS	BS	FK
White	·		3716	◪		930		⌐	3778	W		
3823	⊠		335	▣		955	+		402	S		
746	☐		3354	△		564	⊠		3826		⌐	
745	◇		3350		⌐	563	⊡		841	◙		
676	▣		3687	◼		562	G	⌐	839		⌐	
680	◼		211	▣		561		⌐	452	◼		
3855	✳		209	◼		3813	U		762	☐		
3854	⁙		3746	✤		3817	▣		318	N		
758	▬		519	▣		3816	▣		414	★		
352	▣		517	◧		3774	▣		317		⌐	●
350	◎		3752	Z		3773	H		3799	◼	⌐	●
349		●										

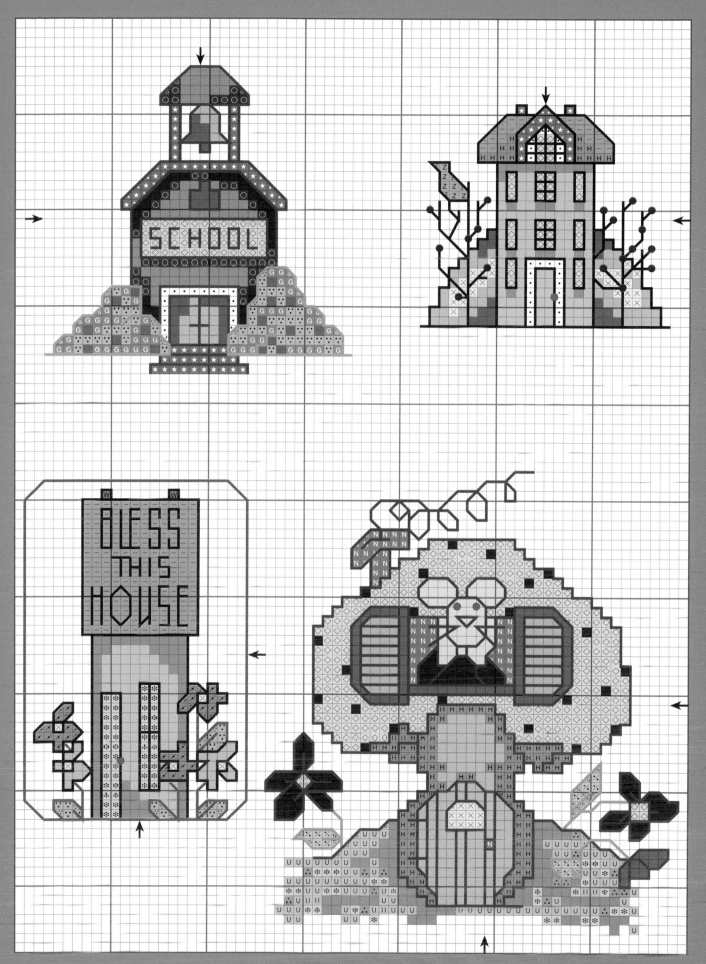

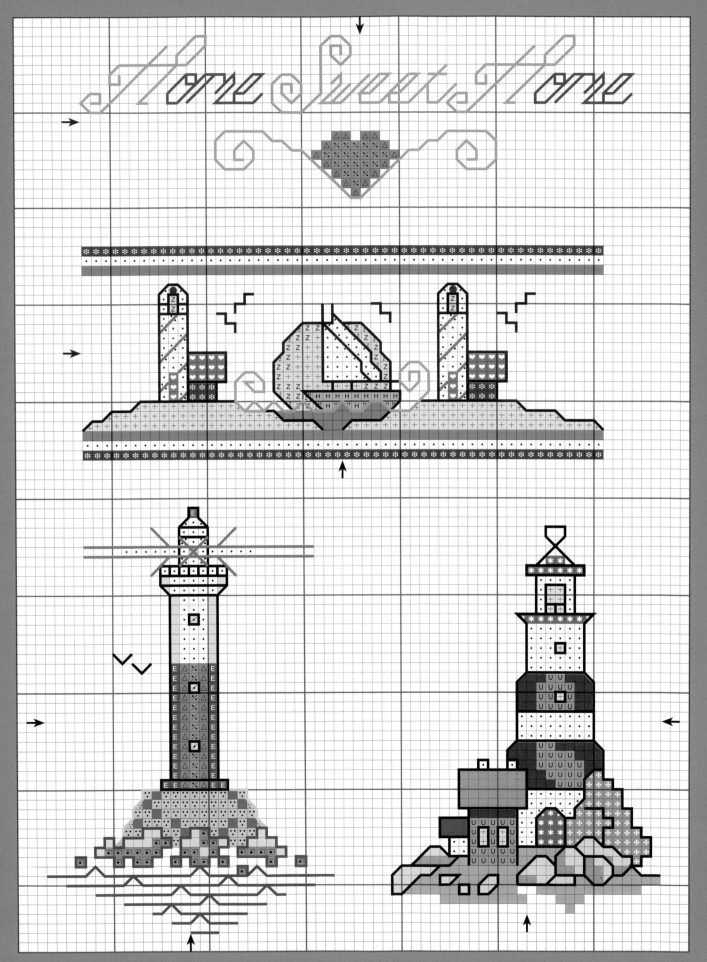

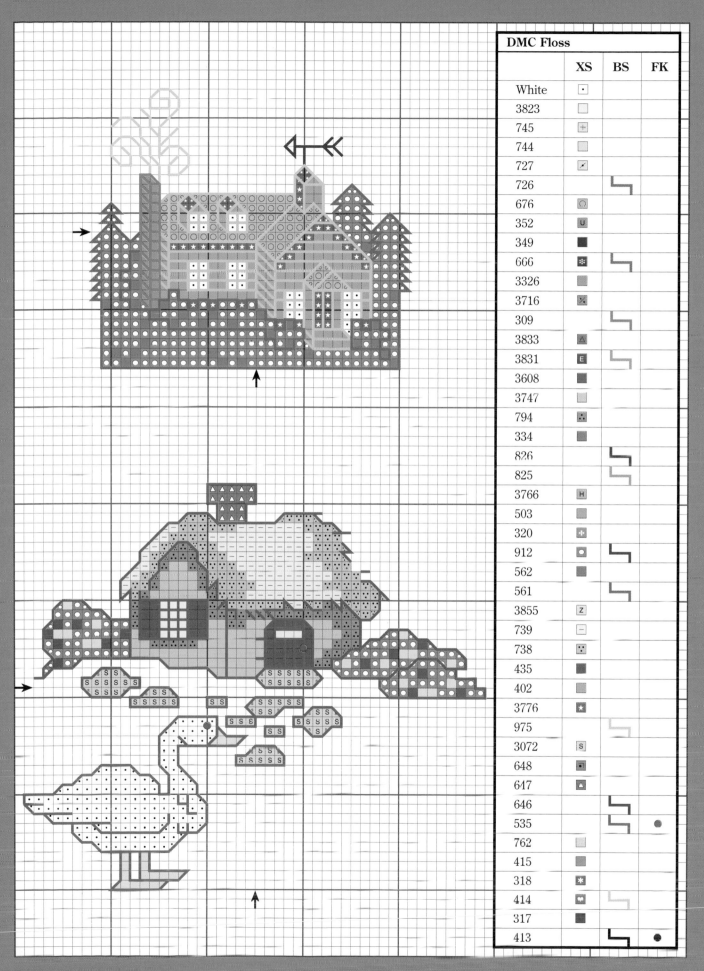

DMC Floss			
	XS	BS	FK
White	·		
3823			
745	+		
744			
727	✗		
726		⌐	
676	Ω		
352	U		
349	■		
666	❋	⌐	
3326			
3716	✗		
309		⌐	
3833	△		
3831	E	⌐	
3608	■		
3747			
794	∴		
334	■		
826		⌐	
825		⌐	
3766	H		
503			
320	✚		
912	◉	⌐	
562	■		
561		⌐	
3855	Z		
739	–		
738	∴		
435	■		
402			
3776	★		
975		⌐	
3072	S		
648	·		
647	▲		
646		⌐	
535		⌐	●
762			
415			
318	❋		
414	◨		
317	■		
413		⌐	●

DMC Floss			
	XS	**BS**	**FK**
White	·		
744			
742	+		
776			
899	O		
335			
326	✚	⌐	●
957	▨		
961	E		
956	W	⌐	●
211			
210	△		
209			
775			
826		⌐	
794	⠢		
334			
964	Z		
959			
3812		⌐	●
772			
703		⌐	
913	⊡	⌐	
912		⌐	
564	╱		
562		⌐	
561		⌐	
3813	U		
3816	★		
991		⌐	●
739	−		
738			
436	S		
3827	⠢		
402	H		
3776		⌐	
975		⌐	
919		⌐	
3072			
648	●		
3023			
535		⌐	●
415	K		
414		⌐	

90

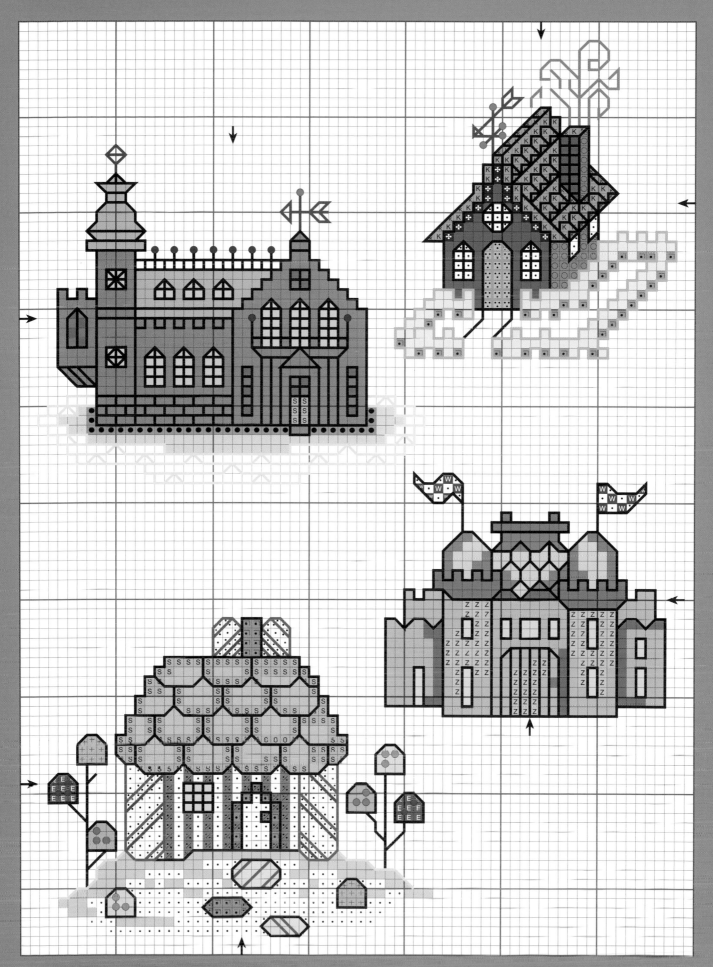

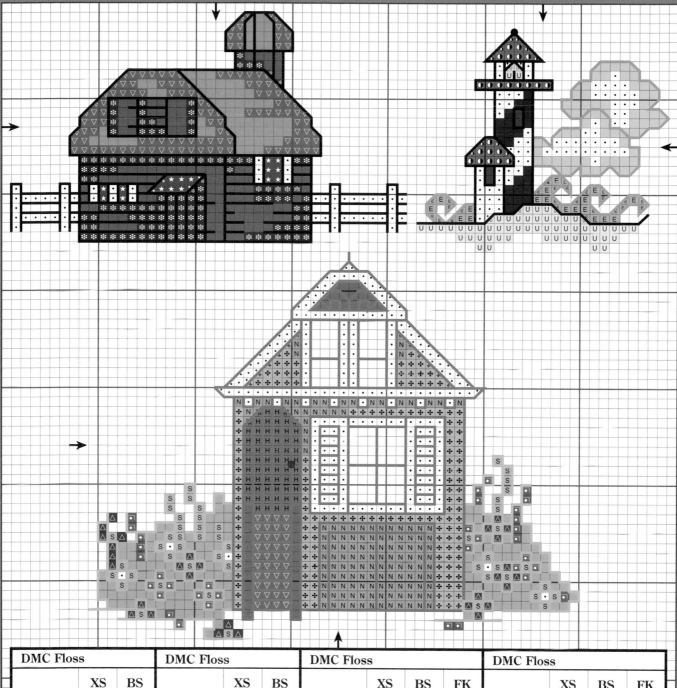

DMC Floss	XS	BS		XS	BS		XS	BS	FK		XS	BS	FK
White	·		3687		⌐	959	E			402	▪		
3078	▫		223	▪		772	▫			977	N		
745	◪		3721	❋		564	½			3776	▪		
742	S		210	▪		563	▪			407	H		
677	⌧		209	▣		561		⌐		632		⌐	●
3822		⌐	775	▫		3812		⌐	●	3864	K		
729		⌐	800	⣿		3810		⌐		415	▪		
945	—		3755	◎		739	U			318	▽		
351	▪		826		⌐	738	▪			414	◨		
350	▲		799		⌐	3855	7			317	★		●
349	▪		3761	+		3827	✦			3799	▪	⌐	●
3689	▪												

DMC Floss			
	XS	BS	FK
White	·		
3078	□		
745	◢		
951	▢		
945	▬		
3064	■		
351	■		
776	▢		
778	✛		
3831		⌐	
309		⌐	
304	■		
223	◉		
3722	▣		
775	▢		
800	⁒		●
3755	△		
334	■		
322		⌐	
828	Z		
827	✛		
3765		⌐	
3760		⌐	
312		⌐	
3761	⊠		
964	⦂		
959	■		
806	★	⌐	●
3813	U		
3816	H		
563	K		
562	◑		
561		⌐	
739	◇		
738	❈		
632		⌐	
647	W		
415	▢		
414	▲		
317		⌐	●
413	■	⌐	

DMC Floss			
	XS	**BS**	**FK**
White	·		
746			
745	−		
3855	⊠		
741	■	⌐	
947	◎		
948			
754	◪		
776	+		
3833	■		
3831		⌐	
3689	◇		
3688	✚		
666	■		
3722	▣		
816	★		
775			
334	▨		
825	■	⌐	●
912	■		
561	◗	⌐	
437	U		
3854	M		
3827	✳		
976	E	⌐	
975			
407	H		
3772	■		
762			
415	■		
318	◧	⌐	
317	■	⌐	●

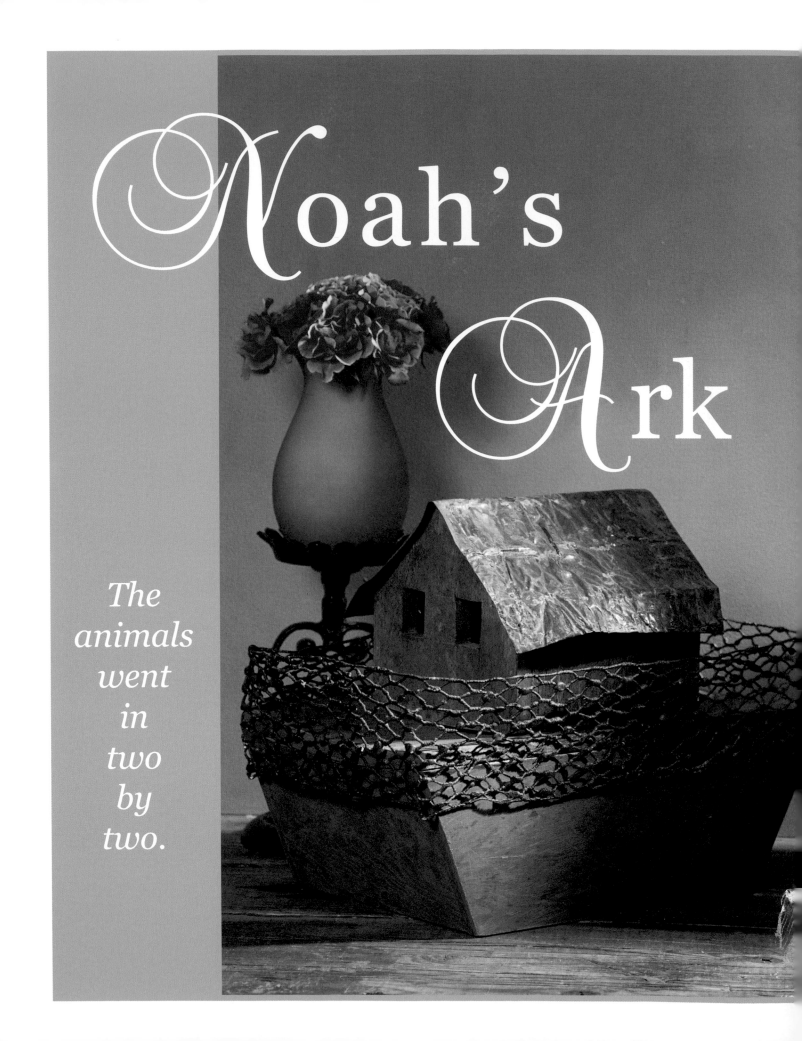

Noah's Ark

The animals went in two by two.

Noah's Ark Sampler

DMC Floss	XS	BS	FK	DMC Floss	XS	BS	FK
White	·			964	▪		
Ecru	×			3766	••		
3078	▫			958	★	⌐	
726	△	⌐		772	▫		
3821	▪			369	⚹		
945	−			368	▽		
758	⚹			704	J		
3341	+	⌐		703	▪	⌐	
3340	▪			562	✤	⌐	
970	✳	⌐		561	■	⌐	
353	⦂			739	◇		
963	▫			738	Z		
957	▪			402	N		
956	E			3776	♥		
606	%	⌐		842	S		
309		⌐		841	▪		
321	■			3773	▪		
816	◉	⌐	●	3772	◨		
211	▫			3858	■	⌐	●
209	▪			762	▫		
554	◎			415	H		
553		⌐		318	⠿		
775	□			414	▪		
800	U			413	W	⌐	●
799	▪			310	◼	⌐	●
312	M	⌐					

The anir

God set my
RAINBOW
in the
clouds
Gen. 9:13

nals came two by two

DMC Floss				DMC Floss			
	XS	BS	FK		XS	BS	FK
White	·			964	▣		
Ecru	⊠			3766	••		
3078	▢			958	★	⌐	
726	△	⌐		772	▢		
3821	▦			369	✗		
945	▬			368	▽		
758	✗			704	J		
3341	+	⌐		703	▦	⌐	
3340	▦			562	✜	⌐	
970	✳	⌐		561	▦	⌐	
353	∴			739	◇		
963	▢			738	Z		
957	▦			402	N		
956	E			3776	♥		
606	▨	⌐		842	S		
309	▦	⌐		841	▦		
321	■			3773	▦		
816	◉	⌐	●	3772	▣		
211	▦			3858	■	⌐	●
209	▦			762	▢		
554	◔			415	H		
553	▦	⌐		318	▦		
775	▢			414	▦		
800	U			413	W	⌐	●
799	▦			310	▣	⌐	●
312	M	⌐					

...and God remembered Noah ...

... and every living

thing·Gen 8:1·

DMC Floss	XS	BS	FK
White	·		
Ecru	×		
3078	☐		
726	△	⌐	
3821	■		
945	–		
758	◪		
3341	✚	⌐	
3340	■		
970	✳	⌐	
353	⁘		
963	■		
957	■		
956	E		
606	▨	⌐	
309	■	⌐	
321	■		
816	◕	⌐	●
211	■		
209	■		
554	◎		
553	■	⌐	
775	☐		
800	U		
799	■	⌐	
312	M	⌐	

DMC Floss	XS	BS	FK
964	■		
3766	••		
958	★	⌐	
772	■		
369	◪		
368	▽		
704	J		
703	■	⌐	
562	✚	⌐	
561	■	⌐	
739	◇		
738	Z		
402	N		
3776	♥		
842	S		
841	■		
3773	■		
3772	◪		
3858	■	⌐	●
762	☐		
415	H		
318	⁘		
414	■		
413	W	⌐	●
310	◪	⌐	●

Bottom Left

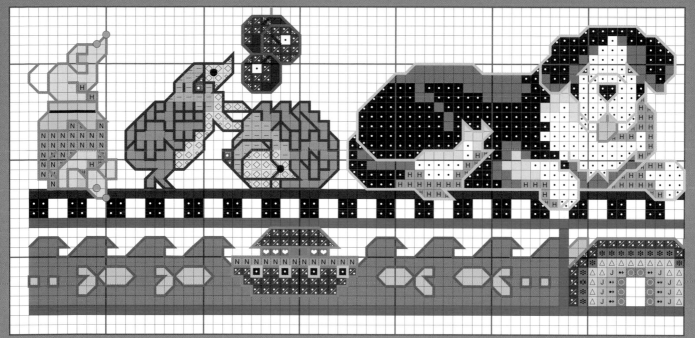

Bottom Center

Bottom Right

DMC Floss	XS	BS	FK	DMC Floss	XS	BS	FK
White	·			964	■		
Ecru	✕			3766	••		
3078	☐			958	★	⌐	
726	△	⌐		772	☐		
3821	■			369	✗		
945	−			368	▽		
758	◣			704	J		
3341	+	⌐		703	■	⌐	
3340	■			562	✚	⌐	
970	✳	⌐		561	■	⌐	
353	⦂			739	◇		
963	■			738	Z		
957	■			402	N		
956	E			3776	♥		
606	▨	⌐		842	S		
309		⌐		841	■		
321	■			3773	■		
816	◙	⌐	●	3772	▣		
211	■			3858	■	⌐	●
209	■			762	☐		
554	◙			415	H		
553		⌐		318	▨		
775	▫			414	■		
800	U			413	W	⌐	●
799	■			310	▪	⌐	●
312	M	⌐					

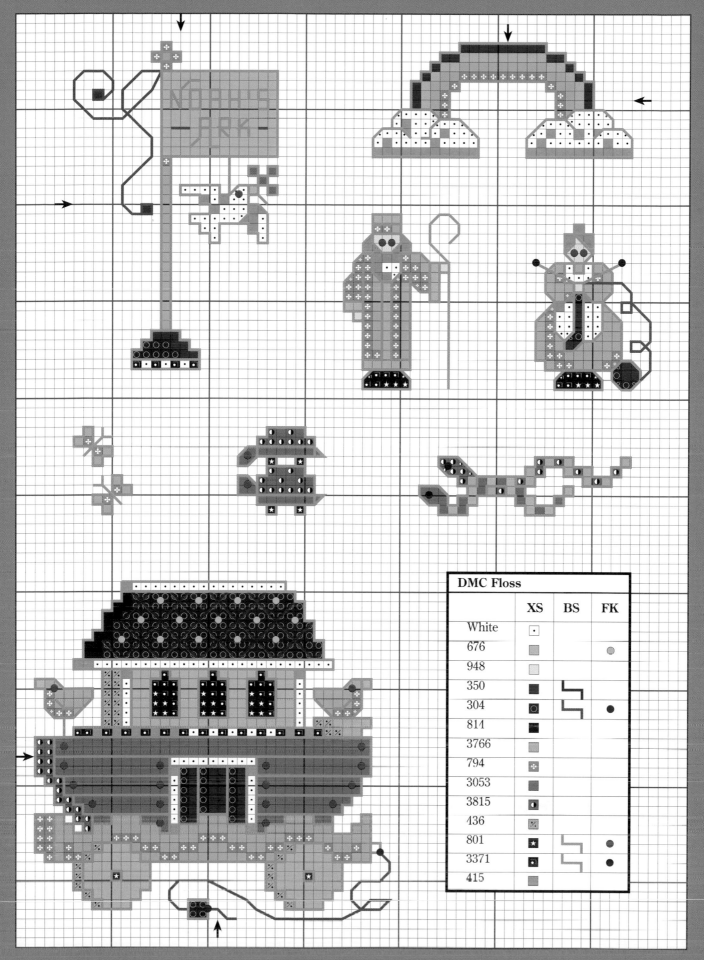

DMC Floss			
	XS	**BS**	**FK**
White	·		
676			●
948			
350		⌐	
304	⊙		●
814			
3766			
794	✚		
3053			
3815	◑		
436	▨		
801	★	⌐	●
3371	▣	⌐	●
415			

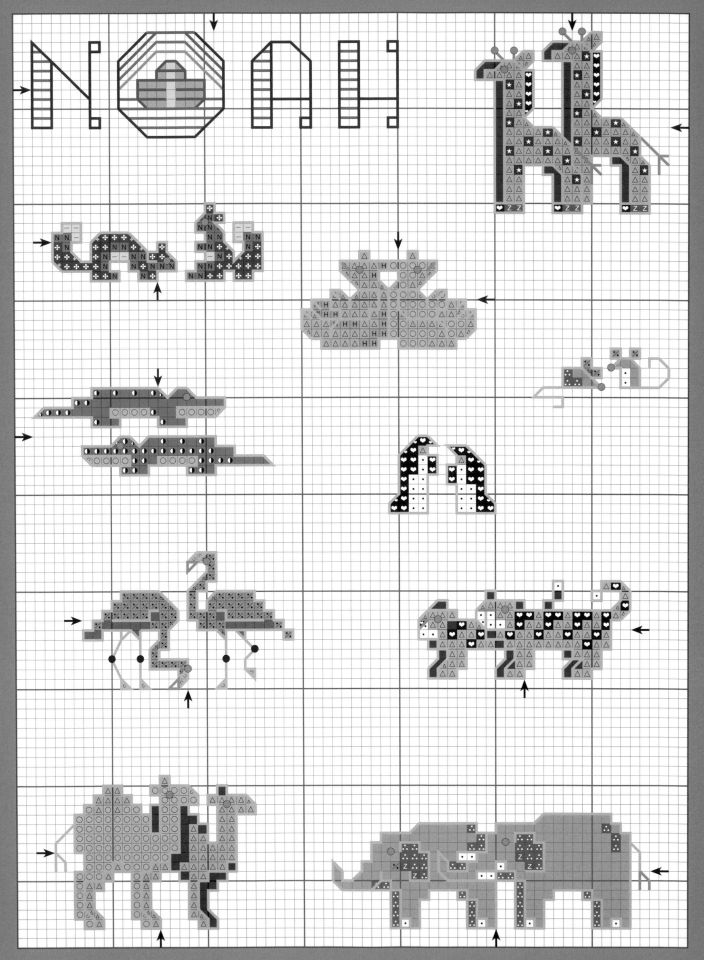

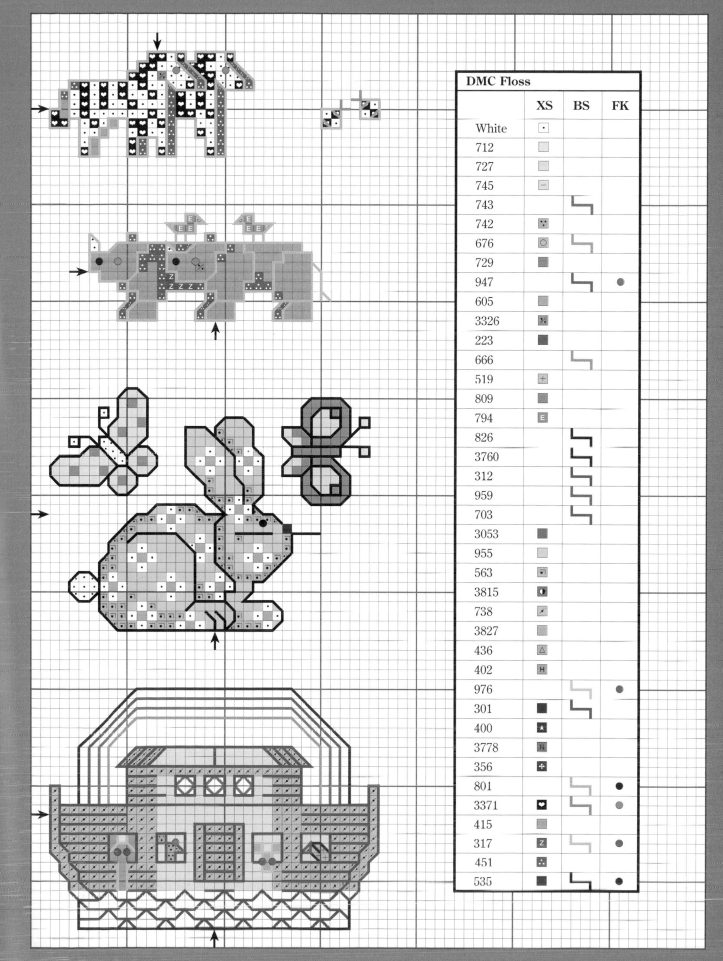

DMC Floss			
	XS	BS	FK
White	·		
712			
727			
745	−		
743		⌐	
742	∴		
676	○	⌐	
729			
947		⌐	●
605			
3326	✖		
223			
666		⌐	
519	✛		
809			
794	E		
826		⌐	
3760		⌐	
312		⌐	
959		⌐	
703		⌐	
3053	■		
955			
563	▣		
3815	◑		
738	◪		
3827			
436	△		
402	H		
976		⌐	●
301	■	⌐	
400	▲		
3778	N		
356	✛		
801		⌐	●
3371	♥	⌐	●
415			
317	Z	⌐	●
451	∷		
535	■	⌐	●

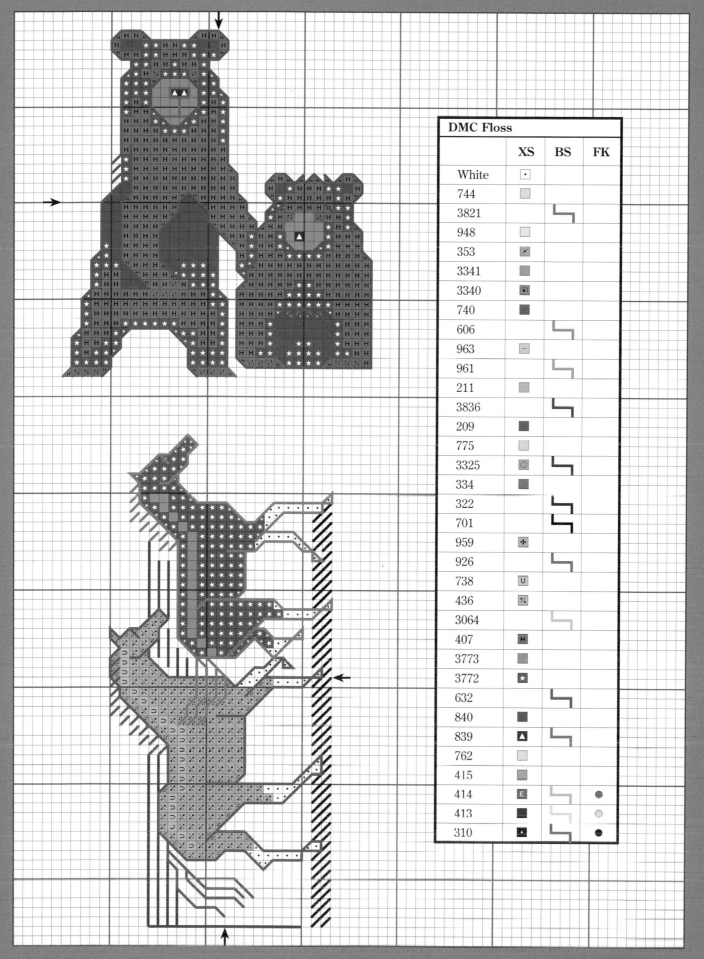

DMC Floss			
	XS	BS	FK
White	·		
744			
3821		⌐	
948			
353	◪		
3341			
3340	⊡		
740	▪		
606		⌐	
963	⚊		
961		⌐	
211			
3836		⌐	
209	▪		
775			
3325	○	⌐	
334	▪		
322		⌐	
701		⌐	
959	✛		
926		⌐	
738	U		
436	◪		
3064		⌐	
407	H		
3773	▪		
3772	✦		
632		⌐	
840	▪		
839	▲	⌐	
762			
415			
414	E	⌐	●
413	▪	⌐	○
310	▣	⌐	●

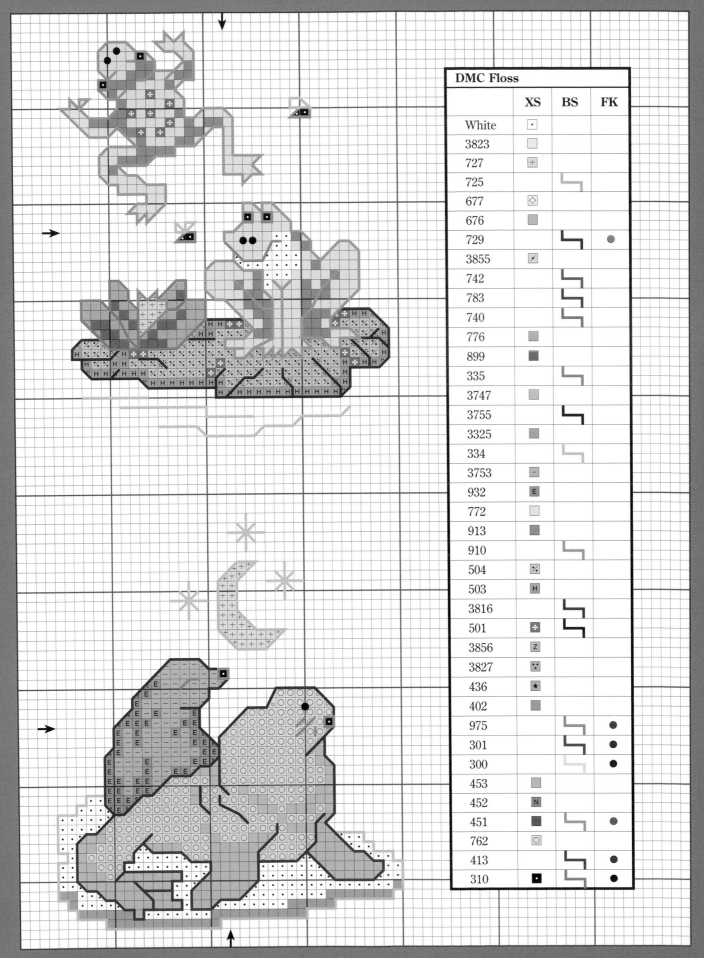

DMC Floss			
	XS	**BS**	**FK**
White	·		
3823			
727	+		
725		⌐	
677	◇		
676			
729		⌐	●
3855	◢		
742		⌐	
783		⌐	
740		⌐	
776			
899			
335		⌐	
3747			
3755		⌐	
3325			
334		⌐	
3753	—		
932	E		
772			
913			
910		⌐	
504	％		
503	H		
3816		⌐	
501	✛	⌐	
3856	Z		
3827	⠿		
436	★		
402			
975		⌐	●
301		⌐	●
300		⌐	●
453			
452	N		
451		⌐	●
762	○		
413		⌐	●
310	■	⌐	●

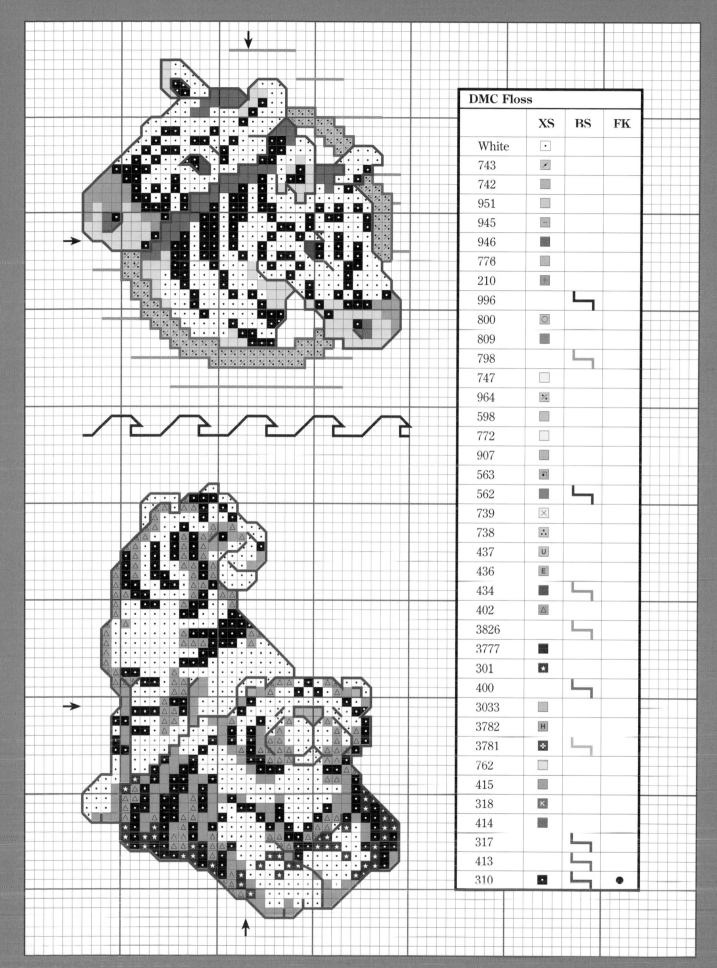

DMC Floss			
	XS	BS	FK
White	·		
743	⊿		
742	▨		
951	▨		
945	⊟		
946	▦		
778	▨		
210	⊞		
996		⌐	
800	○		
809	▨		
798		⌐	
747	▢		
964	⊠		
598	▨		
772	▢		
907	▨		
563	⊡		
562	▦	⌐	
739	⊠		
738	∴		
437	U		
436	E		
434	▦	⌐	
402	△		
3826		⌐	
3777	▦		
301	★		
400		⌐	
3033	▨		
3782	H		
3781	✧	⌐	
762	▢		
415	▨		
318	K		
414	▦		
317		⌐	
413		⌐	
310	⊡	⌐	●

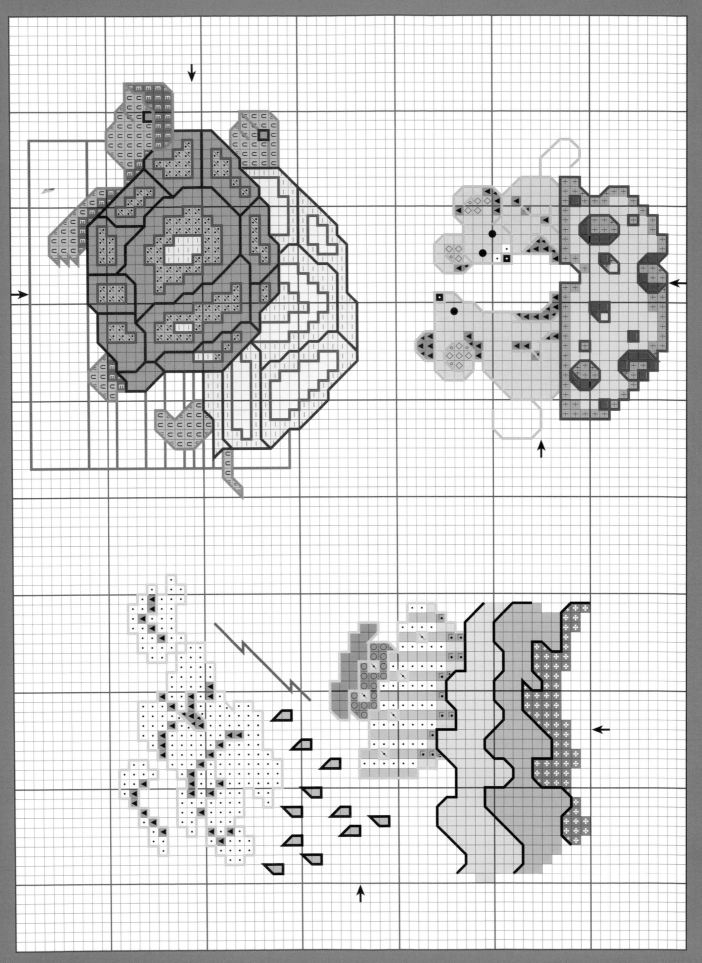

DMC Floss			
	XS	**BS**	**FK**
White	·		
746			
727			
726		⌐	
677	−		
676			
729		⌐	
3770			
3341	◎		
741			
3825	+		
721			
963	◇		
210			
3756			
775			
800			
3755		⌐	
809	✛		
322			
798		⌐	
312		⌐	
3348			
3053	E		
987		⌐	
955			
954			
3813	U		
3815		⌐	
402			
3776			
921		⌐	
301		⌐	
3782			
3828		⌐	
420		⌐	
3781		⌐	
762			
415	▲		
413		⌐	
310	■	⌐	●

DMC Floss			
	XS	**BS**	**FK**
White	·		
822	☐		
744	+		
743	▨		
725		⌐	
783		⌐	
740		⌐	
353	−		
761	△		
3706	▨		
3731		⌐	
3350		⌐	
3836		⌐	
775	▨		
3325	◎		
794		⌐	●
813		⌐	
964	▨		
3348	▨		
369	∴		
966	▨		
912	▨		
562		⌐	
986		⌐	
739	✕		
3827	E		
3773	▨		
3826		⌐	
975	★	⌐	
632	▨	⌐	
762	☐		
415	✣		
414	▨	⌐	
413		⌐	●

stuvwxyz abcdef
ghijklmnopqrstuvwxyz

ABCDEFGHIJK
LMNOPQRSTU
VWXYZ 123456
7890 ABCDEFG
HIJKLMNOPQR
STUVWXYZ

1234567890

ABCDEFGHI
JKLMNOPQR
STUVWXYZ

Anchor Conversion Chart

DMC	Anchor	DMC	Anchor	DMC	Anchor	DMC	Anchor	DMC	Anchor
B5200	1	371	887	580	924	734	279	824	164
White	2	372	887	581	281	738	361	825	162
Ecru	387	400	351	597	1064	739	366	826	161
208	110	402	1047	598	1062	740	316	827	160
209	109	407	914	600	59	741	304	828	9159
210	108	413	236	601	63	742	303	829	906
211	342	414	235	602	57	743	302	830	277
221	897	415	398	603	62	744	301	831	277
223	895	420	374	604	55	745	300	832	907
224	893	422	372	605	1094	746	275	833	874
225	1026	433	358	606	334	747	158	834	874
300	352	434	310	608	330	754	1012	838	1088
301	1049	435	365	610	889	758	9575	839	1086
304	19	436	363	611	898	760	1022	840	1084
307	289	437	362	612	832	761	1021	841	1082
309	42	444	291	613	831	762	234	842	1080
310	403	445	288	632	936	772	259	844	1041
311	148	451	233	640	393	775	128	869	375
312	979	452	232	642	392	776	24	890	218
315	1019	453	231	644	391	778	968	891	35
316	1017	469	267	645	273	780	309	892	33
317	400	470	266	646	8581	781	308	893	27
318	235	471	265	647	1040	782	308	894	26
319	1044	472	253	648	900	783	307	895	1044
320	215	498	1005	666	46	791	178	898	380
321	47	500	683	676	891	792	941	899	38
322	978	501	878	677	361	793	176	900	333
326	59	502	877	680	901	794	175	902	897
327	101	503	876	699	923	796	133	904	258
333	119	504	206	700	228	797	132	905	257
334	977	517	162	701	227	798	146	906	256
335	40	518	1039	702	226	799	145	907	255
336	150	519	1038	703	238	800	144	909	923
340	118	520	862	704	256	801	359	910	230
341	117	522	860	712	926	806	169	911	205
347	1025	523	859	718	88	807	168	912	209
349	13	524	858	720	325	809	130	913	204
350	11	535	401	721	324	813	161	915	1029
351	10	543	933	722	323	814	45	917	89
352	9	550	101	725	305	815	44	918	341
353	8	552	99	726	295	816	43	919	340
355	1014	553	98	727	293	817	13	920	1004
356	1013	554	95	729	890	818	23	921	1003
367	216	561	212	730	845	819	271	922	1003
368	214	562	210	731	281	820	134	924	851
369	1043	563	208	732	281	822	390	926	850
370	888	564	206	733	280	823	152	927	849

DMC	Anchor	DMC	Anchor	DMC	Anchor	DMC	Anchor	Variegated Colors	
928	274	3021	905	3722	1027	3816	876		
930	1035	3022	8581	3726	1018	3817	875	48	1207
931	1034	3023	899	3727	1016	3818	923	51	1220
932	1033	3024	388	3731	76	3819	278	52	1209
934	862	3031	905	3733	75	3820	306	53	——
935	861	3032	898	3740	872	3821	305	57	1203
936	846	3033	387	3743	869	3822	295	61	1218
937	268	3041	871	3746	1030	3823	386	62	1201
938	381	3042	870	3747	120	3824	8	67	1212
939	152	3045	888	3750	1036	3825	323	69	1218
943	189	3046	887	3752	1032	3826	1049	75	1206
945	881	3047	852	3753	1031	3827	311	90	1217
946	332	3051	845	3755	140	3828	373	91	1211
947	330	3052	844	3756	1037	3829	901	92	1215
948	1011	3053	843	3760	162	3830	5975	93	1210
950	4146	3064	883	3761	928			94	1216
951	1010	3072	397	3765	170			95	1209
954	203	3078	292	3766	167			99	1204
955	203	3325	129	3768	779			101	1213
956	40	3326	36	3770	1009			102	1209
957	50	3328	1024	3772	1007			103	1210
958	187	3340	329	3773	1008			104	1217
959	186	3341	328	3774	778			105	1218
961	76	3345	268	3776	1048			106	1203
962	75	3346	267	3777	1015			107	1203
963	23	3347	266	3778	1013			108	1220
964	185	3348	264	3779	868			111	1218
966	240	3350	77	3781	1050			112	1201
970	925	3354	74	3782	388			113	1210
971	316	3362	263	3787	904			114	1213
972	298	3363	262	3790	904			115	1206
973	290	3364	261	3799	236			121	1210
975	357	3371	382	3801	1098			122	1215
976	1001	3607	87	3802	1019			123	——
977	1002	3608	86	3803	69			124	1210
986	246	3609	85	3804	63			125	1213
987	244	3685	1028	3805	62			126	1209
988	243	3687	68	3806	62				
989	242	3688	75	3807	122				
991	1076	3689	49	3808	1068				
992	1072	3705	35	3809	1066				
993	1070	3706	33	3810	1066				
995	410	3708	31	3811	1060				
996	433	3712	1023	3812	188				
3011	856	3713	1020	3813	875				
3012	855	3716	25	3814	1074				
3013	853	3721	896	3815	877				

Metric Conversion Chart

mm-millimetres cm-centimetres
inches to millimetres and centimetres

inches	mm	cm	inches	cm	inches	cm
⅛	3	0.3	9	22.9	30	76.2
¼	6	0.6	10	25.4	31	78.7
⅜	10	1.0	11	27.9	32	81.3
½	13	1.3	12	30.5	33	83.8
⅝	16	1.6	13	33.0	34	86.4
¾	19	1.9	14	35.6	35	88.9
⅞	22	2.2	15	38.1	36	91.4
1	25	2.5	16	40.6	37	94.0
1¼	32	3.2	17	43.2	38	96.5
1½	38	3.8	18	45.7	39	99.1
1¾	44	4.4	19	48.3	40	101.6
2	51	5.1	20	50.8	41	104.1
2½	64	6.4	21	53.3	42	106.7
3	76	7.6	22	55.9	43	109.2
3½	89	8.9	23	58.4	44	111.8
4	102	10.2	24	61.0	45	114.3
4½	114	11.4	25	63.5	46	116.8
5	127	12.7	26	66.0	47	119.4
6	152	15.2	27	68.6	48	121.9
7	178	17.8	28	71.1	49	124.5
8	203	20.3	29	73.7	50	127.0

Index